The Agricola and Germany of Tacitus, and The Dialogue on Oratory

UNIVERSITY OF CALIFORNIA, SAN DIEGO
3 1822 02361 4092

THE

AGRICOLA AND GERMANY OF TACITUS,

AND

THE DIALOGUE ON ORATORY.

THE AGRICOLA AND GERMANY OF TACITUS,

AND

THE DIALOGUE ON ORATORY

TRANSLATED INTO ENGLISH

WITH NOTES AND MAPS

BY

ALFRED JOHN CHURCH, M.A.,

OF LINCOLN COLLEGE, OXFORD; HEAD-MASTER OF KING EDWARD'S SCHOOL, RETFORD;

AND

WILLIAM JACKSON BRODRIBB, M.A.,

LATE FELLOW OF ST. JOHN'S COLLEGE, CAMBRIDGE

(*REVISED* 1877.)

London:

MACMILLAN AND CO.

1885.

LONDON
R. CLAY, SONS, AND TAYLOR,
BREAD STREET HILL, E.C.

CONTENTS.

PREFACE.

THE favourable reception which was given to our translation of the "History" of Tacitus encouraged us to undertake the work which we now present to our readers. We have sought, as before, to make our version such as may satisfy scholars who demand a faithful rendering of the original, and English readers who are offended by the baldness and frigidity which commonly disfigure translations Our task has been made unusually difficult by the style of our author, which is even beyond his wont harsh and obscure, and by the frequently corrupt state of the text, offering as it does sometimes a variety of meanings equally unacceptable, and sometimes none at all.

To critics who accuse us of wanting original genius we have no defence to offer We will only say that they must exercise considerable patience if they are to wait till great writers undertake a work which brings neither fame nor profit. The practical hints and suggestions which have been given us from various quarters we have endeavoured to turn to good account. The classical student will, we trust, appreciate our efforts to express the meaning of our author, though he may often dissent from our opinions. And we hope that the general reader will find an attraction in our subject. Englishmen may well feel an interest in an important passage of the history of our island and in the description of the primitive life of a kindred people, even when these are presented in the uninviting form of a translation.

THE present edition, which we have revised with considerable care and, we hope, with a satisfactory result, contains a translation of the "Dialogus de Oratoribus," a brief essay on oratory in general, and more particularly on the supposed decline of Roman oratory in the Flavian age. Although it is, we believe, rarely read, it has a certain amount of interest, as it touches on the Roman education of the period and its special faults and weaknesses. The Roman youth, it seems, was in many respects strikingly like our own, and parts of the work might have been appropriately written in our own day. It is thoroughly worth reading, and the tradition which has attributed it to Tacitus, though called in question by some scholars and critics, appears to be on the whole a reasonable one.

A. J. C.
W. J. B.

ADVERTISEMENT.

THE "Dialogue about Famous Orators" concludes a task which has occupied much of our time for nearly twenty years past,—the translation of the *Works of Tacitus* To give with sufficient faithfulness an author's meaning is now, with all the aids that a translator can command, comparatively easy. To furnish the English reader with anything like an adequate representation of the style and genius of the original must ever be in the highest degree difficult. It requires, besides a special aptitude for the work, such an expenditure of time and labour as only the amplest leisure could supply. If the work of translation could have a share in the proposed "endownment of research," it might be possible to reach an ideal to which those who have to live by their work can but distantly aspire. Meanwhile we have to acknowledge much kind and generous approbation of our work, and much valuable and instructive criticism. Of this, when it has dealt with details, we have often availed ourselves. When we have been told in more general terms that we ought to be more forcible, more faithful, or more free, we have been obliged to be content with acknowledging the excellence of the advice, and regretting that we were not able to follow it.

A. J. C.
W. J. B.

RETFORD,
July 4, 1877.

INTRODUCTION TO THE LIFE OF CNÆUS JULIUS AGRICOLA.

THE life of Agricola was probably published some time between the October of the year 97 A.D. and the 23rd of January, A.D. 98. This seems fairly inferred from the opening words of ch. 3, in which Tacitus implies, by the omission of the title "Divus," that Nerva Cæsar was still living, and speaks of Trajan as "now daily augmenting the prosperity of the time." Nerva adopted Trajan in October, A.D. 97, and died the 23rd of January in the following year. Orelli indeed refers the publication to the beginning of Trajan's reign, on the ground that the brief period of three months, during which he was associated with Nerva in the empire, would hardly justify Tacitus in praising him more highly than Nerva during the lifetime of the latter. Again, he says, Trajan was in Germany, and did not come to Rome till Nerva's death. These arguments fail to convince us. Tacitus says of Nerva that, "at the very beginning of a most happy age, he blended things once irreconcilable, sovereignty and freedom." This surely is very high praise,—quite as high, we think, as that bestowed on

Trajan. "But Trajan was not at Rome at that time." He was, in fact, giving proofs of his ability as a commander on the Rhine, in the province of Lower Germany, perhaps the most trying and responsible position in which a Roman could be placed. He was elected to share the empire not only by the voice of Nerva, but by that of the Senate and people. His absence from Rome, under such circumstances, seems no reason for supposing that what is said of him is not perfectly applicable to this particular time.

The purpose of his work, Tacitus tells us, was to do honour to Agricola. He exhibits him as the great general of the age, as the Roman who first thoroughly explored and conquered Britain To have achieved this difficult work was, no doubt, in the judgment of Tacitus, Agricola's chief claim to distinction. His glory culminated in his great victory over the Caledonian tribes at the foot of the "Mons Grampius" Comparatively little is told us about his boyhood and youth, and very little about the last eight years of his life. It is plainly hinted that he fell a victim to the jealousy of Domitian. This was the popular impression at the time, and Dion Cassius, the only writer besides Tacitus who speaks of Agricola, accepts it as a certainty.

As a specimen of ancient biography, executed by a man of remarkable genius, the Life of Agricola has always been much read and admired Both father-in-law and son-in-law appear equally to advantage. Of himself, Tacitus speaks with graceful modesty; of his illustrious father-in-law in affectionate, and at the same time judicious, terms of admiration. There is no fulsome or overstrained panegyric The author praises indeed highly and warmly, but in calm and dignified language. In the touching and beautiful conclusion to which the work is brought in the last three chapters, he combines the noblest eloquence with the most perfect good taste. His narrative throughout is striking and vivid, and tells much in a brief compass Nothing could be more impressive than the description of the defeat and overthrow of the confederated Caledonian tribes, and of the terrible scenes presented by the battle-field. The speeches, too, of Galgacus and Agricola seem to be in the very best style of Tacitus. They are not merely eloquent and stirring; they also skilfully reflect, on the one hand, the passionate and impulsive fury of the barbarian, and, on the other, the calm confidence of the Roman general in the firmness and sense of honour of his well-trained and hitherto victorious legionaries.

The Life of Agricola, though frequently read from the interest of its subject-matter, and its completeness in itself, is by no means easy, and is ill-suited to young scholars. It has, we think, an almost disproportionate share of the peculiar difficulties of Tacitus. Our notes show that it contains several crabbed and obscure passages. Unfortunately, too, the text is in an unsatisfactory state. There are three or four passages, at least, in which no ingenuity on the part of critics has much chance of restoring the original. Wex, in his elaborate edition, published in 1852, has fully discussed every difficulty of reading and interpretation, and has suggested many emendations. We have always consulted, and sometimes followed, him. We have also made use of Kritz's edition, published in 1859. This is, in fact, a recension of Wex, whose text, with some variations, he adopts. His notes are much shorter, and are well adapted to the ordinary student They are sensible and useful. This, we believe, is the most recent edition of the Agricola.

The geography of Ancient Britain is not so intricate as that of Germany; but the Agricola raises questions which are by no means free from difficulty. It is easy to follow the campaigns of the first two summers, A.D. 78 and A.D. 79. In A.D. 78 Agricola crushed the Ordovices, who occupied North Wales, and pursued them into Anglesey. In A.D. 79 he invaded the territory of the Brigantes, and conquered the country north of the Humber. The following year brought him into contact with hitherto unknown tribes, and saw him advance as far as the Taus or Tanaus. This cannot have been the Frith of Tay, as it seems clear, from ch 23, that he had not as yet penetrated so far north. Dr. Merivale[1] thinks it is

[1] Hist of Romans, ch lxi

the Frith of Forth,—nearly the same, in fact, as Bodotria, the one being the estuary, the other the river. It has been suggested that it may have been the mouth of the Tweed, or that of the North Tyne at Dunbar. This last hypothesis we think to be the most probable. In this case Agricola would have overrun that portion of Scotland which is to the south of the Friths of Clyde and Forth. These are, respectively, Clota and Bodotria. The fourth summer was passed in the consolidation of his conquests; in the fifth, he advanced northwards into Dumbarton and Argyle, as it would appear from ch. 24, in which Ireland is mentioned; in the sixth, he invaded the regions to the north of the Frith of Forth, so that Fife, Stirling, and perhaps Perth and Forfar, must have been the scene of the campaign. His army was accompanied by a fleet. In the following year, A.D. 84, was fought the great battle with the Caledonian tribes under Galgacus, the site of which has been the subject of endless conjectures. We think with Dr. Merivale that it may be presumed to have been at no very great distance from the coast, since it is implied that the army and fleet were acting together. He is inclined to place it in the neighbourhood of Forfar or Brechin. It may have been as far north as Aberdeen or Banff

Summer being now over, Agricola retired with his army into the territory of the Boresti, or Horesti, as the name is written in the best MSS Where this was is wholly uncertain; no author but Tacitus mentions them Probably their settlements were to the north of the Frith of Forth, as we are not told that Agricola recrossed Bodotria. Meanwhile the fleet was ordered to sail round Britain. We are told that it eventually entered "the harbour of Trutulium," from which it appears to have started for its voyage Tacitus, however, is here obscure from his conciseness The name Trutulium occurs nowhere else One would suppose from the context that it could not have been at any great distance from Bodotria. Very possibly it was somewhere on the coast of Fife.

Tacitus no doubt refers to this voyage when he says, in ch. 10, "Round these coasts of remotest ocean the Roman fleet then, for the first time, sailed, and ascertained that Britain is an island." It does not follow that he meant to say that the Romans actually circumnavigated Britain on this occasion. It is enough to suppose that they sailed from the Frith of Forth along the eastern coast as far as Cape Wrath, the north-western extremity. They would thus pass through the Pentland Frith, and see the Orkney, possibly the Shetland, Islands When they found that the coast made a sharp bend southwards, they would be convinced that Britain was an island. This seems the simplest and most probable view of the matter, and it is adopted by Mannert and Dr. Merivale,[1] both of whom reject the notion of a complete circumnavigation of Britain, though Dion Cassius[2] implies that it was accomplished. There is no real difficulty about the word "circumvehi," which Tacitus uses, and which, at first sight, might seem to demand such a meaning. "Circumvehi," as Dr. Merivale remarks, may signify simply "to make a sweep," or "to be wafted from point to point"

If this view is correct, the somewhat obscure words at the end of ch. 38, "proximo Britanniæ latere lecto omni," will mean "after having skirted all the nearest," *i.e.* the east coast of Caledonia.

[1] Hist. of Romans, ch. lxi See note.
[2] Dion Cass. apud Xiphil lxvi. 20.

CHRONOLOGICAL SUMMARY OF THE ROMAN EXPEDITIONS INTO BRITAIN FROM CAIUS JULIUS CÆSAR TO CNÆUS JULIUS AGRICOLA.

CAIUS JULIUS CÆSAR twice invaded Britain, in B.C. 55 and B.C. 54.

The next expedition was not till the reign of the Emperor Claudius, who, A.D. 43, sent Aulus Plautius, under whom served Vespasian. Claudius, soon after, followed in person, defeated the Trinobantes, under their chief Caractacus, and conquered the southern portion of Britain. He received from the Senate the cognomen of Britannicus, A.D. 44. Aulus Plautius and Vespasian remained in Britain. Plautius was recalled to Rome A.D. 47, and was succeeded by Ostorius Scapula. Scapula completely crushed the Silures, overthrew Caractacus in a great battle (probably on the Clun in Shropshire), and founded the colony of Camulodunum (Colchester), A.D. 50 Aulus Didius succeeded Scapula as proprætor of Britain A.D. 52. He did little to advance the Roman dominion. Veranius was governor for one uneventful year, A.D. 58 He was succeeded by Suetonius Paulinus, A.D. 59, who crushed the great insurrection of the Iceni under Boudicea, A.D. 61. Petronius Turpilianus was the next governor, A.D. 62. There were now two years of peace, and Roman civilization began to find its way into Britain.

Trebellius Maximus was governor from A.D. 65 to 69; Vettius Bolanus from A.D. 69 to 70; Petilius Cerialis from A.D. 70 to 75; and Julius Frontinus from A.D. 75 to 78. Agricola then succeeded as "legatus consularis."

MAP TO ILLUSTRATE THE AGRICOLA OF TACITUS

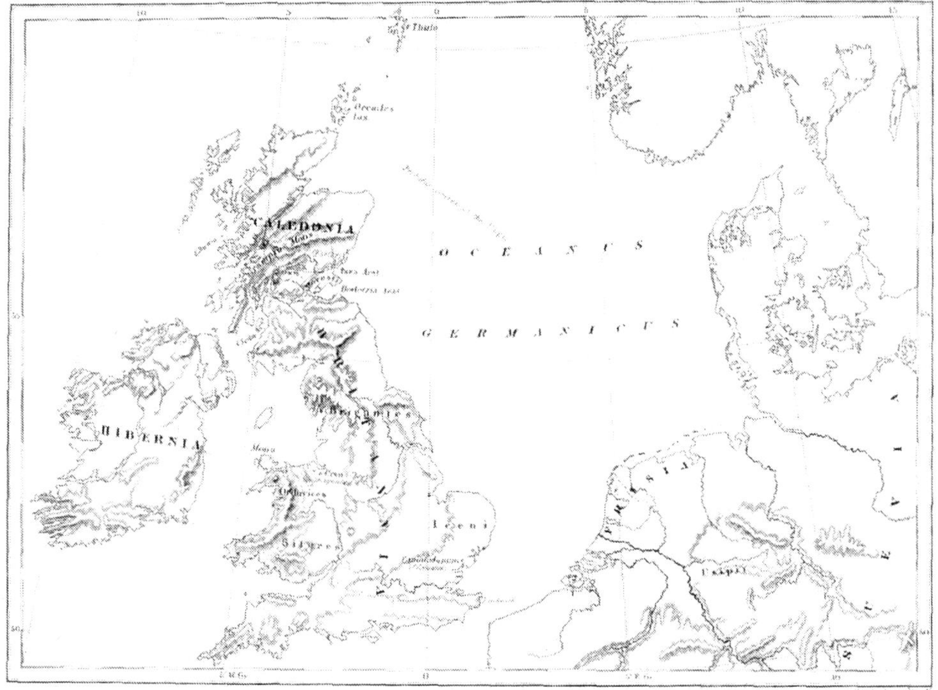

London & Cambridge; Macmillan & Co.

THE LIFE OF

CNÆUS JULIUS AGRICOLA.

Biography of great men; its dangers in a bad age

To bequeath to posterity a record of the deeds and characters of distinguished men is an ancient practice which even the present age, careless as it is of its own sons, has not abandoned whenever some great and conspicuous excellence has conquered and risen superior to that failing, common to petty and to great states, blindness and hostility to goodness. But in days gone by, as there was a greater inclination and a more open path to the achievement of memorable actions, so the man of highest genius was led by the simple reward of a good conscience to hand on without partiality or self-seeking the remembrance of greatness. Many too thought that to write their own lives showed the confidence of integrity rather than presumption Of Rutilius and Scaurus no one doubted the honesty or questioned the motives So true is it that merit is best appreciated by the age in which it thrives most easily. But in these days, I, who have to record the life of one who has passed away, must crave an indulgence, which I should not have had CHAP. I

CHAP. I. to ask had I only to inveigh against an age so cruel, so hostile to all virtue.

CHAP II We have read that the panegyrics pronounced by Arulenus Rusticus on Pætus Thrasea, and by Herennius Senecio on Priscus Helvidius, were made capital crimes, that not only their persons but their very books were objects of rage, and that the triumvirs were commissioned to burn in the forum those works of splendid genius They fancied, forsooth, that in that fire the voice of the Roman people, the freedom of the Senate, and the conscience of the human race were perishing, while at the same time they banished the teachers of philosophy, and exiled every noble pursuit, that nothing good might anywhere confront them. Certainly we showed a magnificent example of patience; as a former age had witnessed the extreme of liberty, so we witnessed the extreme of servitude, when the informer robbed us of the interchange of speech and hearing. We should have lost memory as well as voice, had it been as easy to forget as to keep silence.

Biography difficult even in a happier time

CHAP III Now at last our spirit is returning. And yet, though at the dawn of a most happy age Nerva Cæsar blended things once irreconcilable, sovereignty and freedom, though Nerva Trajan is now daily augmenting the prosperity of the time, and though the public safety has not only our hopes and good wishes, but has also the certain pledge of their fulfilment, still, from the necessary condition of human frailty, the remedy works less quickly than the disease. As

CHAP II

our bodies grow but slowly, perish in a moment, so it is easier to crush than to revive genius and its pursuits. Besides, the charm of indolence steals over us, and the idleness which at first we loathed we afterwards love. What if during those fifteen years, a large portion of human life, many were cut off by ordinary casualties, and the ablest fell victims to the Emperor's rage, if a few of us survive, I may almost say, not only others but our ownselves, survive, though there have been taken from the midst of life those many years which brought the young in dumb silence to old age, and the old almost to the very verge and end of existence! Yet we shall not regret that we have told, though in language unskilful and unadorned, the story of past servitude, and borne our testimony to present happiness. Meanwhile this book, intended to do honour to Agricola, my father-in-law, will, as an expression of filial regard, be commended, or at least excused.

A.D. 40. *Birth, parentage, and education of Agricola.*

CHAP IV

Cnæus Julius Agricola was born at the ancient and famous colony of Forum Julii.[1] Each of his grandfathers was an Imperial procurator, that is, of the highest equestrian rank. His father, Julius Græcinus, a member of the Senatorian order, and distinguished for his pursuit of eloquence and philosophy, earned for himself by these very merits the displeasure of Caius Cæsar. He was ordered to impeach Marcus Silanus, and because he refused was put to death. His mother was Julia Procilla, a lady of singular

[1] Frejus.

CHAP IV virtue. Brought up by her side with fond affection, he passed his boyhood and youth in the cultivation of every worthy attainment. He was guarded from the enticements of the profligate not only by his own good and straightforward character, but also by having, when quite a child, for the scene and guide of his studies, Massilia,[1] a place where refinement and provincial frugality were blended and happily combined. I remember that he used to tell us how in his early youth he would have imbibed a keener love of philosophy than became a Roman and a senator, had not his mother's good sense checked his excited and ardent spirit. It was the case of a lofty and aspiring soul craving with more eagerness than caution the beauty and splendour of great and glorious renown. But it was soon mellowed by reason and experience, and he retained from his learning that most difficult of lessons—moderation.

A.D. 59—62. *ÆT. 20—23. He serves in Britain.*

CHAP V He served his military apprenticeship in Britain to the satisfaction of Suetonius Paullinus, a painstaking and judicious officer, who, to test his merits, selected him to share his tent Without the recklessness with which young men often make the profession of arms a mere pastime, and without indolence, he never availed himself of his tribune's rank or his inexperience to procure enjoyment or to escape from duty. He sought to make himself acquainted with the province and known to the army; he would learn from the skilful, and keep pace with the bravest, would

[1] Marseilles.

attempt nothing for display, would avoid nothing from fear, and would be at once careful and vigilant. CHAP. V

Never indeed had Britain been more excited, or in a more critical condition. Veteran soldiers had been massacred, colonies burnt, armies cut off. The struggle was then for safety; it was soon to be for victory. And though all this was conducted under the leadership and direction of another, though the final issue and the glory of having won back the province belonged to the general, yet skill, experience, and ambition were acquired by the young officer. His soul too was penetrated with the desire of warlike renown, a sentiment unwelcome to an age which put a sinister construction on eminent merit, and made glory as perilous as infamy.

A.D. 62—68. *ÆT.* 23—29. *His Marriage. He becomes Quæstor and Prætor.*

From Britain he went to Rome, to go through the regular course of office, and there allied himself with Domitia Decidiana, a lady of illustrious birth. The marriage was one which gave a man ambitious of advancement distinction and support. They lived in singular harmony, through their mutual affection and preference of each other to self. However, the good wife deserves the greater praise, just as the bad incurs a heavier censure. CHAP. VI

Appointed Quæstor, the ballot gave him Asia for his province, Salvius Titianus for his proconsul. Neither the one nor the other corrupted him, though the province was rich and an easy prey to the wrong-doer, while the proconsul, a man inclined to every

CHAP. VI. species of greed, was ready by all manner of indulgence to purchase a mutual concealment of guilt.

A daughter was there added to his family to be his stay and comfort, for shortly after he lost the son that had before been born to him. The year between his quæstorship and tribunate, as well as the year of the tribunate itself, he passed in retirement and inaction, for he knew those times of Nero when indolence stood for wisdom. His prætorship was passed in the same consistent quietude, for the usual judicial functions did not fall to his lot. The games and the pageantry of his office he ordered according to the mean between strictness and profusion, avoiding extravagance, but not missing distinction. He was afterwards appointed by Galba to draw up an account of the temple offerings, and his searching scrutiny relieved the conscience of the state from the burden of all sacrileges but those committed by Nero.

A.D 69—70. *ÆT.* 30—31. *Death of his Mother. He espouses the cause of Vespasian and is appointed to the command of the 20th Legion*

CHAP. VII The following year inflicted a terrible blow on his affections and his fortunes. Otho's fleet, while cruising idly about, cruelly ravaged Intemelii,[1] a district of Liguria; his mother, who was living here on her own estate, was murdered. The estate itself and a large part of her patrimony were plundered This was indeed the occasion of the crime. Agricola, who instantly set out to discharge the duties of affection,

[1] Vintimiglia.

was overtaken by the tidings that Vespasian was aiming at the throne. He at once joined his party. Vespasian's early policy, and the government of Rome were directed by Mucianus, for Domitian was a mere youth, and from his father's elevation sought only the opportunities of indulgence. CHAP. VII.

Agricola, having been sent by Mucianus to conduct a levy of troops, and having done his work with integrity and energy, was appointed to command the 20th Legion, which had been slow to take the new oath of allegiance, and the retiring officer of which was reported to be acting disloyally. It was a trying and formidable charge for even officers of consular rank, and the late prætorian officer, perhaps from his own disposition, perhaps from that of the soldiers, was powerless to restrain them. Chosen thus at once to supersede and to punish, Agricola, with a singular moderation, wished it to be thought that he had found rather than made an obedient soldiery.

A.D. 72. *ÆT.* 33. *He continues to serve in Britain with increasing distinction.*

Britain was then under Vettius Bolanus, who governed more mildly than suited so turbulent a province Agricola moderated his energy and restrained his ardour, that he might not grow too important, for he had learnt to obey, and understood well how to combine expediency with honour. Soon afterwards Britain received for its governor a man of consular rank, Petilius Cerialis Agricola's merits had now room for display. Cerialis let him share at first indeed only the toils and dangers, but before long CHAP. VIII.

CHAP VIII the glory of war, often by way of trial putting him in command of part of the army, and sometimes, on the strength of the result, of larger forces Never to enhance his own renown did Agricola boast of his exploits; he always referred his success, as though he were but an instrument, to his general and director. Thus by his valour in obeying orders and by his modesty of speech he escaped jealousy without losing distinction.

A.D. 73—78. *ÆT.* 34—39. *He is ennobled, becomes Governor of Aquitania, is recalled to Rome to be made Consul.*

CHAP IX As he was returning from the command of the legion, Vespasian admitted him into the patrician order, and then gave him the province of Aquitania, a pre-eminently splendid appointment both from the importance of its duties and the prospect of the consulate to which the Emperor destined him. Many think the genius of the soldier wants subtlety, because military law, which is summary and blunt, and apt to appeal to the sword, finds no exercise for the refinements of the forum Yet Agricola, from his natural good sense, though called to act among civilians, did his work with ease and correctness. And, besides, the times of business and relaxation were kept distinct. When his public and judicial duties required it, he was dignified, thoughtful, austere, and yet often merciful, when business was done with, he wore no longer the official character. He was altogether without harshness, pride, or the greed of gain. With a most rare felicity, his good nature did not weaken his authority, nor his strictness the attachment of his friends. To speak of uprightness and purity in such a man would be an insult to his virtues. Fame itself, of which even good men are often weakly fond, he did not seek by an ostentation of virtue or by artifice. He avoided rivalry with his colleagues, contention with his procurator, thinking such victories no honour and defeat disgrace. For somewhat less than three years he was kept in his governorship, and was then recalled with an immediate prospect of the consulate. A general belief went with him that the province of Britain was to be his, not because he had himself hinted it, but because he seemed worthy of it. Public opinion is not always mistaken; sometimes even it chooses the right man. He was consul, and I but a youth, when he betrothed to me his daughter, a maiden even then of noble promise. After his consulate he gave her to me in marriage, and was then at once appointed to the government of Britain, with the addition of the sacred office of the pontificate. CHAP. IX

Britain; its boundaries, shape, and surrounding seas.

The geography and inhabitants of Britain, already described by many writers, I will speak of, not that my research and ability may be compared with theirs, but because the country was then for the first time thoroughly subdued. And so matters, which as being still not accurately known my predecessors embellished with their eloquence, shall now be related on the evidence of facts. CHAP X

Britain, the largest of the islands which Roman geography includes, is so situated that it faces Germany on the east, Spain on the west; on the south it is even within sight of Gaul; its northern extremities, which have no shores opposite to them, are beaten by the waves of a vast open sea. The form of the entire country has been compared by Livy and Fabius Rusticus, the most graphic among ancient and modern historians, to an oblong shield or battle-axe. And this no doubt is its shape without Caledonia, so that it has become the popular description of the whole island. There is, however, a large and irregular tract of land which juts out from its furthest shores, tapering off in a wedge-like form. Round these coasts of remotest ocean the Roman fleet then for the first time sailed, ascertained that Britain is an island, and simultaneously discovered and conquered what are called the Orcades, islands hitherto unknown. Thule too was descried in the distance, which as yet had been hidden by the snows of winter. Those waters, they say, are sluggish, and yield with difficulty to the oar, and are not even raised by the wind as other seas. The reason, I suppose, is that lands and mountains, which are the cause and origin of storms, are here comparatively rare, and also that the vast depths of that unbroken expanse are more slowly set in motion. But to investigate the nature of the ocean and the tides is no part of the present work, and many writers have discussed the subject. I would simply add, that nowhere has the sea a wider dominion, that it has many currents running in every direction, that it does not merely flow and ebb within the limits of the shore, but penetrates and winds far inland, and finds a home among hills and mountains as though in its own domain. CHAP. X

Origin of the inhabitants (of Britain).

Who were the original inhabitants of Britain, whether they were indigenous or foreign, is, as usual among barbarians, little known. Their physical characteristics are various, and from these conclusions may be drawn. The red hair and large limbs of the inhabitants of Caledonia point clearly to a German origin. The dark complexion of the Silures, their usually curly hair, and the fact that Spain is the opposite shore to them, are an evidence that Iberians of a former date crossed over and occupied these parts Those who are nearest to the Gauls are also like them, either from the permanent influence of original descent, or, because in countries which run out so far to meet each other, climate has produced similar physical qualities. But a general survey inclines me to believe that the Gauls established themselves in an island so near to them. Their religious belief may be traced in the strongly-marked British superstition. The language differs but little; there is the same boldness in challenging danger, and, when it is near, the same timidity in shrinking from it. The Britons, however, exhibit more spirit, as being a people whom a long peace has not yet enervated. Indeed we have understood that even the Gauls were once renowned in war; but, after a while, sloth following on ease crept over them, and they lost their courage along with CHAP. XI

CHAP. XI. their freedom. This too has happened to the long-conquered tribes of Britain; the rest are still what the Gauls once were.

Military customs; climate; products of the soil.

CHAP XII Their strength is in infantry. Some tribes fight also with the chariot. The higher in rank is the charioteer; the dependants fight. They were once ruled by kings, but are now divided under chieftains into factions and parties. Our greatest advantage in coping with tribes so powerful is that they do not act in concert. Seldom is it that two or three states meet together to ward off a common danger. Thus, while they fight singly, all are conquered.

Their sky is obscured by continual rain and cloud. Severity of cold is unknown. The days exceed in length those of our part of the world; the nights are bright, and in the extreme north so short that between sunlight and dawn you can perceive but a slight distinction. It is said that, if there are no clouds in the way, the splendour of the sun can be seen throughout the night, and that he does not rise and set, but only crosses the heavens. The truth is, that the low shadow thrown from the flat extremities of the earth's surface does not raise the darkness to any height, and the night thus fails to reach the sky and stars.

With the exception of the olive and vine, and plants which usually grow in warmer climates, the soil will yield, and even abundantly, all ordinary produce. It ripens indeed slowly, but is of rapid growth, the cause in each case being the same, namely, the excessive moisture of the soil and of the atmosphere. Britain contains gold and silver and other metals, as the prize of conquest. The ocean, too, produces pearls, but of a dusky and bluish hue. Some think that those who collect them have not the requisite skill, as in the Red Sea the living and breathing pearl is torn from the rocks, while in Britain they are gathered just as they are thrown up. I could myself more readily believe that the natural properties of the pearls are in fault than our keenness for gain. CHAP XII.

Roman Governors of Britain.

The Britons themselves bear cheerfully the conscription, the taxes, and the other burdens imposed on them by the Empire, if there be no oppression. Of this they are impatient; they are reduced to subjection, not as yet to slavery. The deified Julius, the very first Roman who entered Britain with an army, though by a successful engagement he struck terror into the inhabitants and gained possession of the coast, must be regarded as having indicated rather than transmitted the acquisition to future generations. Then came the civil wars, and the arms of our leaders were turned against their country, and even when there was peace, there was a long neglect of Britain. This Augustus spoke of as policy, Tiberius as an inherited maxim. That Caius Cæsar meditated an invasion of Britain is perfectly clear, but his purposes, rapidly formed, were easily changed, and his vast attempts on Germany had failed. Claudius was the first to renew the attempt, and conveyed over into the island some legions and auxiliaries, choosing Vespasian to share with him the campaign, whose CHAP. XIII

CHAP XIII approaching elevation had this beginning. Several tribes were subdued and kings made prisoners, and destiny learnt to know its favourite.

Roman Governors of Britain.

CHAP XIV Aulus Plautius was the first governor of consular rank, and Ostorius Scapula the next Both were famous soldiers, and by degrees the nearest portions of Britain were brought into the condition of a province, and a colony of veterans was also introduced. Some of the states were given to king Cogidumnus, who lived down to our day a most faithful ally. So was maintained the ancient and long-recognised practice of the Roman people, which seeks to secure among the instruments of dominion even kings themselves. Soon after, Didius Gallus consolidated the conquests of his predecessors, and advanced a very few positions into parts more remote, to gain the credit of having enlarged the sphere of government. Didius was succeeded by Veranius, who died within the year. Then Suetonius Paullinus enjoyed success for two years; he subdued several tribes and strengthened our military posts. Thus encouraged, he made an attempt on the island of Mona, as a place from which the rebels drew reinforcements; but in doing this he left his rear open to attack.

Preparations of the Britains for revolt.

CHAP XV. Relieved from apprehension by the legate's absence, the Britons dwelt much among themselves on the miseries of subjection, compared their wrongs, and exaggerated them in the discussion. "All we get by patience," they said, "is that heavier demands are exacted from us, as from men who will readily submit. A single king once ruled us; now two are set over us; a legate to tyrannise over our lives, a procurator to tyrannise over our property. Their quarrels and their harmony are alike ruinous to their subjects. The centurions of the one, the slaves of the other, combine violence with insult. Nothing is now safe from their avarice, nothing from their lust. In war it is the strong who plunders; now, it is for the most part by cowards and poltroons that our homes are rifled, our children torn from us, the conscription enforced, as though it were for our country alone that we could not die. For, after all, what a mere handful of soldiers has crossed over, if we Britons look at our own numbers. Germany did thus actually shake off the yoke, and yet its defence was a river, not the ocean. With us, fatherland, wives, parents, are the motives to war; with them, only greed and profligacy. They will surely fly, as did the now deified Julius, if once we emulate the valour of our sires. Let us not be panicstricken at the result of one or two engagements. The miserable have more fury and greater resolution. Now even the gods are beginning to pity us, for they are keeping away the Roman general, and detaining his army far from us in another island. We have already taken the hardest step; we are deliberating. And indeed, in all such designs, to dare is less perilous than to be detected."

Insurrection headed by Boudicea and crushed by Suetonius Paullinus.

CHAP XVI Rousing each other by this and like language, under the leadership of Boudicca, a woman of kingly descent (for they admit no distinction of sex in their royal successions), they all rose in arms. They fell upon our troops, which were scattered on garrison duty, stormed the forts, and burst into the colony itself, the head-quarters, as they thought, of tyranny. In their rage and their triumph, they spared no variety of a barbarian's cruelty. Had not Paullinus on hearing of the outbreak in the province rendered prompt succour, Britain would have been lost. By one successful engagement, he brought it back to its former obedience, though many, troubled by the conscious guilt of rebellion and by particular dread of the legate, still clung to their arms. Excellent as he was in other respects, his policy to the conquered was arrogant, and exhibited the cruelty of one who was avenging private wrongs. Accordingly Petronius Turpilianus was sent out to initiate a milder rule. A stranger to the enemy's misdeeds and so more accessible to their penitence, he put an end to old troubles, and, attempting nothing more, handed the province over to Trebellius Maximus Trebellius, who was somewhat indolent, and never ventured on a campaign, controlled the province by a certain courtesy in his administration. Even the barbarians now learnt to excuse many attractive vices, and the occurrence of the civil war gave a good pretext for inaction. But we were sorely troubled with mutiny, as troops habituated to service grew demoralised by idleness. Trebellius, who had escaped the soldiers' fury by flying and hiding himself, governed henceforth on sufferance, a disgraced and humbled man. It was a kind of bargain; the soldiers had their licence, the general had his life; and so the mutiny cost no bloodshed. Nor did Vettius Bolanus, during the continuance of the civil wars, trouble Britain with discipline. There was the same inaction with respect to the enemy, and similar unruliness in the camp, only Bolanus, an upright man, whom no misdeeds made odious, had secured affection in default of the power of control. CHAP XVI

Vigorous policy of Vespasian.

When however Vespasian had restored to unity Britain as well as the rest of the world, in the presence of great generals and renowned armies the enemy's hopes were crushed. They were at once panic-stricken by the attack of Petilius Cerialis on the state of the Brigantes, said to be the most prosperous in the entire province. There were many battles, some by no means bloodless, and his conquests, or at least his wars, embraced a large part of the territory of the Brigantes Indeed he would have altogether thrown into the shade the activity and renown of any other successor; but Julius Frontinus was equal to the burden, a great man as far as greatness was then possible, who subdued by his arms the powerful and warlike tribe of the Silures, surmounting the difficulties of the country as well as the valour of the enemy. CHAP XVII

A.D. 78. *ÆT.* 39 *Splendid successes of Agricola in Britain; his Modesty.*

CHAP XVIII Such was the state of Britain, and such were the vicissitudes of the war, which Agricola found on his crossing over about midsummer. Our soldiers made it a pretext for carelessness, as if all fighting was over, and the enemy were biding their time. The Ordovices, shortly before Agricola's arrival, had destroyed nearly the whole of a squadron of allied cavalry quartered in their territory. Such a beginning raised the hopes of the country, and all who wished for war approved the precedent, and anxiously watched the temper of the new governor. Meanwhile Agricola, though summer was past and the detachments were scattered throughout the province, though the soldiers' confident anticipation of inaction for that year would be a source of delay and difficulty in beginning a campaign, and most advisers thought it best simply to watch all weak points, resolved to face the peril. He collected a force of veterans and a small body of auxiliaries, then as the Ordovices would not venture to descend into the plain, he put himself in front of the ranks to inspire all with the same courage against a common danger, and led his troops up a hill The tribe was all but exterminated.

Well aware that he must follow up the prestige of his arms, and that in proportion to his first success would be the terror of the other tribes, he formed the design of subjugating the island of Mona, from the occupation of which Paullinus had been recalled, as I have already related, by the rebellion of the entire province. But, as his plans were not matured, he had no fleet. The skill and resolution of the general accomplished the passage. With some picked men of the auxiliaries, disencumbered of all baggage, who knew the shallows and had that national experience in swimming which enables the Britons to take care not only of themselves but of their arms and horses, he delivered so unexpected an attack that the astonished enemy who were looking for a fleet, a naval armament, and an assault by sea, thought that to such assailants nothing could be formidable or invincible. And so, peace having been sued for and the island given up, Agricola became great and famous as one who, when entering on his province, a time which others spend in vain display and a round of ceremonies, chose rather toil and danger. Nor did he use his success for self-glorification, or apply the name of campaigns and victories to the repression of a conquered people. He did not even describe his achievements in a laurelled letter. Yet by thus disguising his renown he really increased it, for men inferred the grandeur of his aspirations from his silence about services so great. CHAP. XVIII

Moderation and equity of his government.

Next, with thorough insight into the feelings of his province, and taught also, by the experience of others, that little is gained by conquest if followed by oppression, he determined to root out the causes of war. Beginning first with himself and his dependants, he kept his household under restraint, a thing as hard to many as ruling a province He transacted no CHAP. XIX

CHAP. XIX. public business through freedmen or slaves; no private leanings, no recommendations or entreaties of friends, moved him in the selection of centurions and soldiers, but it was ever the best man whom he thought most trustworthy. He knew everything, but did not always act on his knowledge. Trifling errors he treated with leniency, serious offences with severity. Nor was it always punishment, but far oftener penitence, which satisfied him. He preferred to give office and power to men who would not transgress, rather than have to condemn a transgressor. He lightened the exaction of corn and tribute by an equal distribution of the burden, while he got rid of those contrivances for gain which were more intolerable than the tribute itself. Hitherto the people had been compelled to endure the farce of waiting by the closed granary and of purchasing corn unnecessarily and raising it to a fictitious price. Difficult by-roads and distant places were fixed for them, so that states with a winter-camp close to them had to carry corn to remote and inaccessible parts of the country, until what was within the reach of all became a source of profit to the few.

A.D. 79. *ÆT.* 40 *His energy.*

CHAP. XX. Agricola, by the repression of these abuses in his very first year of office, restored to peace its good name, when, from either the indifference or the harshness of his predecessors, it had come to be as much dreaded as war. When, however, summer came, assembling his forces, he continually showed himself in the ranks, praised good discipline, and kept the stragglers in order.

He would himself choose the position of the camp, himself explore the estuaries and forests. Meanwhile he would allow the enemy no rest, laying waste his territory with sudden incursions, and, having sufficiently alarmed him, would then by forbearance display the allurements of peace. In consequence, many states, which up to that time had been independent, gave hostages, and laid aside their animosities; garrisons and forts were established among them with a skill and diligence with which no newly-acquired part of Britain had before been treated. CHAP XX

He encourages the arts of peace.

The following winter passed without disturbance, and was employed in salutary measures. For, to accustom to rest and repose through the charms of luxury a population scattered and barbarous and therefore inclined to war, Agricola gave private encouragement and public aid to the building of temples, courts of justice and dwelling-houses, praising the energetic, and reproving the indolent. Thus an honourable rivalry took the place of compulsion. He likewise provided a liberal education for the sons of the chiefs, and showed such a preference for the natural powers of the Britons over the industry of the Gauls that they who lately disdained the tongue of Rome now coveted its eloquence. Hence, too, a liking sprang up for our style of dress, and the "toga" became fashionable. Step by step they were led to things which dispose to vice, the lounge, the bath, the elegant banquet. All this in their ignorance, CHAP XXI

CHAP. XXI they called civilization, when it was but a part of their servitude.

A.D. 80. *ÆT.* 41. *Conquests in the north of Britain*

CHAP. XXII The third year of his campaigns opened up new tribes, our ravages on the native population being carried as far as the Taus, an estuary so called. This struck such terror into the enemy that he did not dare to attack our army, harassed though it was by violent storms; and there was even time for the erection of forts. It was noted by experienced officers that no general had ever shown more judgment in choosing suitable positions, and that not a single fort established by Agricola was either stormed by the enemy or abandoned by capitulation or flight. Sorties were continually made; for these positions were secured from protracted siege by a year's supply. So winter brought with it no alarms, and each garrison could hold its own, as the baffled and despairing enemy, who had been accustomed often to repair his summer losses by winter successes, found himself repelled alike both in summer and winter.

Never did Agricola in a greedy spirit appropriate the achievements of others; the centurion and the prefect both found in him an impartial witness of their every action. Some persons used to say that he was too harsh in his reproofs, and that he was as severe to the bad as he was gentle to the good. But his displeasure left nothing behind it; reserve and silence in him were not to be dreaded. He thought it better to show anger than to cherish hatred.

A.D. 81. *ÆT.* 42 *He consolidates his conquests.*

CHAP. XXIII

The fourth summer he employed in securing what he had overrun. Had the valour of our armies and the renown of the Roman name permitted it, a limit to our conquests might have been found in Britain itself. Clota and Bodotria, estuaries which the tides of two opposite seas carry far back into the country, are separated by but a narrow strip of land. This Agricola then began to defend with a line of forts, and, as all the country to the south was now occupied, the enemy were pushed into what might be called another island.

A.D. 82 *ÆT.* 43. *Description of Ireland.*

CHAP. XXIV.

In the fifth year of the war Agricola, himself in the leading ship, crossed the Clota, and subdued in a series of victories tribes hitherto unknown. In that part of Britain which looks towards Ireland, he posted some troops, hoping for fresh conquests rather than fearing attack, inasmuch as Ireland, being between Britain and Spain and conveniently situated for the seas round Gaul, might have been the means of connecting with great mutual benefit the most powerful parts of the empire. Its extent is small when compared with Britain, but exceeds the islands of our seas. In soil and climate, in the disposition, temper, and habits of its population, it differs but little from Britain. We know most of its harbours and approaches, and that through the intercourse of commerce. One of the petty kings of the nation, driven

CHAP. XXIV. out by internal faction, had been received by Agricola, who detained him under the semblance of friendship till he could make use of him. I have often heard him say that a single legion with a few auxiliaries could conquer and occupy Ireland, and that it would have a salutary effect on Britain for the Roman arms to be seen everywhere, and for freedom, so to speak, to be banished from its sight

A.D. 83. *ÆT. 44. He advances north, and is confronted by a general union of the Caledonian tribes.*

CHAP. XXV. In the summer in which he entered on the sixth year of his office, his operations embraced the states beyond Bodotria, and, as he dreaded a general movement among the remoter tribes, as well as the perils which would beset an invading army, he explored the harbours with a fleet, which, at first employed by him as an integral part of his force, continued to accompany him. The spectacle of war thus pushed on at once by sea and land was imposing, while often infantry, cavalry, and marines, mingled in the same encampment and joyously sharing the same meals, would dwell on their own achievements and adventures, comparing, with a soldier's boastfulness, at one time the deep recesses of the forest and the mountain with the dangers of waves and storms, or, at another, battles by land with victories over the ocean. The Britons too, as we learnt from the prisoners, were confounded by the sight of a fleet, as if, now that their inmost seas were penetrated, the conquered had their last refuge closed against them. The tribes inhabiting Caledonia flew

CHAP XXV.

to arms, and with great preparations, made greater by the rumours which always exaggerate the unknown, themselves advanced to attack our fortresses, and thus, challenging a conflict, inspired us with alarm. To retreat south of the Bodotria, and to retire rather than to be driven out, was the advice of timid pretenders to prudence, when Agricola learnt that the enemy's attack would be made with more than one army. Fearing that their superior numbers and their knowledge of the country might enable them to hem him in, he too distributed his forces into three divisions, and so advanced.

CHAP XXVI.

This becoming known to the enemy, they suddenly changed their plan, and with their whole force attacked by night the ninth Legion, as being the weakest, and cutting down the sentries, who were asleep or panic-stricken, they broke into the camp. And now the battle was raging within the camp itself, when Agricola, who had learnt from his scouts the enemy's line of march and had kept close on his track, ordered the most active soldiers of his cavalry and infantry to attack the rear of the assailants, while the entire army were shortly to raise a shout. Soon his standards glittered in the light of daybreak. A double peril thus alarmed the Britons, while the courage of the Romans revived; and feeling sure of safety, they now fought for glory. In their turn they rushed to the attack, and there was a furious conflict within the narrow passages of the gates till the enemy were routed. Both armies did their utmost, the one for the honour of having given aid,

CHAP. XXVI the other for that of not having needed support. Had not the flying enemy been sheltered by morasses and forests, this victory would have ended the war.

Preparations on both sides for further conflict

CHAP XXVII. Knowing this, and elated by their glory, our army exclaimed that nothing could resist their valour—that they must penetrate the recesses of Caledonia, and at length after an unbroken succession of battles, discover the furthest limits of Britain. Those who but now were cautious and prudent, became after the event eager and boastful It is the singularly unfair peculiarity of war that the credit of success is claimed by all, while a disaster is attributed to one alone. But the Britons thinking themselves baffled, not so much by our valour as by our general's skilful use of an opportunity, abated nothing of their arrogant demeanour, arming their youth, removing their wives and children to a place of safety, and assembling together to ratify, with sacred rites, a confederacy of all their states. Thus, with angry feelings on both sides, the combatants parted.

Singular adventures of a Usipian cohort.

CHAP. XXVIII. The same summer a Usipian cohort, which had been levied in Germany and transported into Britain, ventured on a great and memorable exploit. Having killed a centurion and some soldiers, who, to impart military discipline, had been incorporated with their ranks and were employed at once to instruct and command them, they embarked on board three swift galleys with pilots pressed into their service. Under the direction of one of them—for two of the three they suspected and consequently put to death—they sailed past the coast in the strangest way before any rumour about them was in circulation. After a while, dispersing in search of water and provisions, they encountered many of the Britons, who sought to defend their property. Often victorious, though now and then beaten, they were at last reduced to such an extremity of want as to be compelled to eat, at first, the feeblest of their number, and then victims selected by lot. Having sailed round Britain and lost their vessels from not knowing how to manage them, they were looked upon as pirates and were intercepted, first by the Suevi and then by the Frisii. Some who were sold as slaves in the way of trade, and were brought through the process of barter as far as our side of the Rhine, gained notoriety by the disclosure of this extraordinary adventure. CHAP XXVIII

A.D. 84. *ÆT.* 45. *Further advance into Caledonia Union of the Caledonian tribes.*

Early in the summer Agricola sustained a domestic affliction in the loss of a son born a year before, a calamity which he endured, neither with the ostentatious fortitude displayed by many brave men, nor, on the other hand, with womanish tears and grief. In his sorrow he found one source of relief in war Having sent on a fleet, which by its ravages at various points might cause a vague and wide-spread alarm, he advanced with a lightly equipped force, including in its ranks some Britons of remarkable CHAP XXIX

CHAP. XXIX. bravery, whose fidelity had been tried through years of peace, as far as the Grampian mountains, which the enemy had already occupied. For the Britons, indeed, in no way cowed by the result of the late engagement, had made up their minds to be either avenged or enslaved, and convinced at length that a common danger must be averted by union, had, by embassies and treaties, summoned forth the whole strength of all their states. More than 30,000 armed men were now to be seen, and still there were pressing in all the youth of the country, with all whose old age was yet hale and vigorous, men renowned in war and bearing each decorations of his own. Meanwhile, among the many leaders, one superior to the rest in valour and in birth, Galgacus by name, is said to have thus harangued the multitude gathered around him and clamouring for battle:—

Speech of the Caledonian chief, Galgacus.

CHAP. XXX "Whenever I consider the origin of this war and the necessities of our position, I have a sure confidence that this day, and this union of yours, will be the beginning of freedom to the whole of Britain. To all of us slavery is a thing unknown; there are no lands beyond us, and even the sea is not safe, menaced as we are by a Roman fleet And thus in war and battle, in which the brave find glory, even the coward will find safety. Former contests, in which, with varying fortune, the Romans were resisted, still left in us a last hope of succour, inasmuch as being the most renowned nation of Britain, dwelling in the very heart of the country, and out of sight of the shores of the conquered, we could keep even our eyes unpolluted by the contagion of slavery. To us who dwell on the uttermost confines of the earth and of freedom, this remote sanctuary of Britain's glory has up to this time been a defence. Now, however, the furthest limits of Britain are thrown open, and the unknown always passes for the marvellous. But there are no tribes beyond us, nothing indeed but waves and rocks, and the yet more terrible Romans, from whose oppression escape is vainly sought by obedience and submission. Robbers of the world, having by their universal plunder exhausted the land, they rifle the deep. If the enemy be rich, they are rapacious; if he be poor, they lust for dominion; neither the east nor the west has been able to satisfy them. Alone among men they covet with equal eagerness poverty and riches. To robbery, slaughter, plunder, they give the lying name of empire; they make a solitude and call it peace. CHAP. XXX.

"Nature has willed that every man's children and kindred should be his dearest objects. Yet these are torn from us by conscriptions to be slaves elsewhere. Our wives and our sisters, even though they may escape violation from the enemy, are dishonoured under the names of friendship and hospitality. Our goods and fortunes they collect for their tribute, our harvests for their granaries. Our very hands and bodies, under the lash and in the midst of insult, are worn down by the toil of clearing forests and morasses. Creatures born to slavery are sold once for all, and CHAP. XXXI

CHAP XXXI are, moreover, fed by their masters; but Britain is daily purchasing, is daily feeding, her own enslaved people And as in a household the last comer among the slaves is always the butt of his companions, so we in a world long used to slavery, as the newest and the most contemptible, are marked out for destruction. We have neither fruitful plains, nor mines, nor harbours, for the working of which we may be spared. Valour, too, and high spirit in subjects, are offensive to rulers; besides, remoteness and seclusion, while they give safety, provoke suspicion. Since then you cannot hope for quarter, take courage, I beseech you, whether it be safety or renown that you hold most precious Under a woman's leadership the Brigantes were able to burn a colony, to storm a camp, and had not success ended in supineness, might have thrown off the yoke. Let us, then, a fresh and unconquered people, never likely to abuse our freedom, show forthwith at the very first onset what heroes Caledonia has in reserve

CHAP XXXII "Do you suppose that the Romans will be as brave in war as they are licentious in peace? To our strifes and discords they owe their fame, and they turn the errors of an enemy to the renown of their own army, an army which, composed as it is of every variety of nations, is held together by success and will be broken up by disaster. These Gauls and Germans, and, I blush to say, these numerous Britons, who, though they lend their lives to support a stranger's rule, have been its enemies longer than its subjects, you cannot imagine to be bound by fidelity and affection. Fear

CHAP XXXII

and terror there certainly are, feeble bonds of attachment; remove them, and those who have ceased to fear will begin to hate. All the incentives to victory are on our side. The Romans have no wives to kindle their courage; no parents to taunt them with flight; many have either no country or one far away. Few in number, dismayed by their ignorance, looking around upon a sky, a sea, and forests which are all unfamiliar to them; hemmed in, as it were, and enmeshed, the Gods have delivered them into our hands. Be not frightened by idle display, by the glitter of gold and of silver, which can neither protect nor wound. In the very ranks of the enemy we shall find our own forces. Britons will acknowledge their own cause; Gauls will remember past freedom; the other Germans will abandon them, as but lately did the Usipii Behind them there is nothing to dread. The forts are ungarrisoned; the colonies in the hands of aged men; what with disloyal subjects and oppressive rulers, the towns are ill-affected and rife with discord. On the one side you have a general and an army; on the other, tribute, the mines, and all the other penalties of an enslaved people. Whether you endure these for ever, or instantly avenge them, this field is to decide. Think, therefore, as you advance to battle, at once of your ancestors and of your posterity."

Preparations for battle. Agricola's address to his army.

CHAP. XXXIII

They received his speech with enthusiasm, and as is usual among barbarians, with songs, shouts and discordant cries. And now was seen the assembling of troops and the gleam of arms, as the boldest warriors

CHAP. XXXIII.

stepped to the front. As the line was forming, Agricola, who, though his troops were in high spirits and could scarcely be kept within the entrenchments, still thought it right to encourage them, spoke as follows—

"Comrades, this is the eighth year since, thanks to the greatness and good fortune of Rome and to your own loyalty and energy, you conquered Britain. In our many campaigns and battles, whether courage in meeting the foe, or toil and endurance in struggling, I may say, against nature herself, have been needed, I have ever been well satisfied with my soldiers, and you with your commander. And so you and I have passed beyond the limits reached by former armies or by former governors, and we now occupy the last confines of Britain, not merely in rumour and report, but with an actual encampment and armed force. Britain has been both discovered and subdued. Often on the march, when morasses, mountains, and rivers were wearing out your strength, did I hear our bravest men exclaim, 'When shall we have the enemy before us?—when shall we fight?' He is now here, driven from his lair, and your wishes and your valour have free scope, and everything favours the conqueror, everything is adverse to the vanquished. For as it is a great and glorious achievement, if we press on, to have accomplished so great a march, to have traversed forests and to have crossed estuaries, so, if we retire, our present most complete success will prove our greatest danger. We have not the same knowledge of the country or the same abundance of supplies, but we have arms in our hands, and in them we have everything For myself I have long been convinced that neither for an army nor for a general is retreat safe. Better, too, is an honourable death than a life of shame, and safety and renown are for us to be found together. And it would be no inglorious end to perish on the extreme confines of earth and of nature. CHAP. XXXIII.

"If unknown nations and an untried enemy confronted you, I should urge you on by the example of other armies. As it is, look back upon your former honours, question your own eyes. These are the men who last year under cover of darkness attacked a single legion, whom you routed by a shout. Of all the Britons these are the most confirmed runaways, and this is why they have survived so long. Just as when the huntsman penetrates the forest and the thicket, all the most courageous animals rush out upon him, while the timid and feeble are scared away by the very sound of his approach, so the bravest of the Britons have long since fallen; and the rest are a mere crowd of spiritless cowards. You have at last found them, not because they have stood their ground, but because they have been overtaken. Their desperate plight, and the extreme terror that paralyses them, have rivetted their line to this spot, that you might achieve in it a splendid and memorable victory. Put an end to campaigns; crown your fifty years' service with a glorious day; prove to your country that her armies could never have been fairly charged with protracting a war or with causing a rebellion." CHAP. XXXIV.

CHAP. XXXV

Order of the Roman Army.

While Agricola was yet speaking, the ardour of the soldiers was rising to its height, and the close of his speech was followed by a great outburst of enthusiasm. In a moment they flew to arms. He arrayed his eager and impetuous troops in such a manner that the auxiliary infantry, 8,000 in number, strengthened his centre, while 3,000 cavalry were posted on his wings The legions were drawn up in front of the intrenched camp, his victory would be vastly more glorious if won without the loss of Roman blood, and he would have a reserve in case of repulse. The enemy, to make a formidable display, had posted himself on high ground; his van was on the plain, while the rest of his army rose in an arch-like form up the slope of a hill. The plain between resounded with the noise and with the rapid movements of chariots and cavalry. Agricola, fearing that from the enemy's superiority of force he would be simultaneously attacked in front and on the flanks, widened his ranks, and though his line was likely to be too extended, and several officers advised him to bring up the legions, yet, so sanguine was he, so resolute in meeting danger, he sent away his horse and took his stand on foot before the colours.

The battle.

CHAP. XXXVI

The action began with distant fighting. The Britons with equal steadiness and skill used their huge swords and small shields to avoid or to parry the missiles of our soldiers, while they themselves poured on us a dense shower of darts, till Agricola encouraged three Batavian and two Tungrian cohorts to bring matters to the decision of close fighting with swords. Such tactics were familiar to these veteran soldiers, but were embarrassing to an enemy armed with small bucklers and unwieldy weapons. The swords of the Britons are not pointed, and do not allow them to close with the foe, or to fight in the open field No sooner did the Batavians begin to close with the enemy, to strike them with their shields, to disfigure their faces, and overthrowing the force on the plain to advance their line up the hill, than the other auxiliary cohorts joined with eager rivalry in cutting down all the nearest of the foe. Many were left behind half dead, some even unwounded, in the hurry of victory. Meantime the enemy's cavalry had fled, and the charioteers had mingled in the engagement of the infantry. But although these at first spread panic, they were soon impeded by the close array of our ranks and by the inequalities of the ground. The battle had anything but the appearance of a cavalry action, for men and horses were carried along in confusion together, while chariots, destitute of guidance, and terrified horses without drivers, dashed as panic urged them, sideways, or in direct collision against the ranks. CHAP. XXXVI.

Defeat of the Britons. Loss on both sides.

Those of the Britons who, having as yet taken no part in the engagement, occupied the hill-tops, and who without fear for themselves sat idly disdaining the smallness of our numbers, had begun gradually CHAP. XXXVII

CHAP XXXVII

to descend and to hem in the rear of the victorious army, when Agricola, who feared this very movement, opposed their advance with four squadrons of cavalry held in reserve by him for any sudden emergencies of battle. Their repulse and rout was as severe as their onset had been furious. Thus the enemy's design recoiled on himself, and the cavalry which by the general's order had wheeled round from the van of the contending armies, attacked his rear. Then, indeed, the open plain presented an awful and hideous spectacle. Our men pursued, wounded, made prisoners of the fugitives only to slaughter them when others fell in their way And now the enemy, as prompted by their various dispositions, fled in whole battalions with arms in their hands before a few pursuers, while some, who were unarmed, actually rushed to the front and gave themselves up to death. Everywhere there lay scattered arms, corpses, and mangled limbs, and the earth reeked with blood. Even the conquered now and then felt a touch of fury and of courage. On approaching the woods, they rallied, and as they knew the ground, they were able to pounce on the foremost and least cautious of the pursuers. Had not Agricola, who was present everywhere, ordered a force of strong and lightly-equipped cohorts, with some dismounted troopers for the denser parts of the forest, and a detachment of cavalry where it was not so thick, to scour the woods like a party of huntsmen, serious loss would have been sustained through the excessive confidence of our troops. When, however, the enemy saw that we again pursued them in firm and compact array, they fled no longer in masses as before, each looking for his comrade; but dispersing and avoiding one another, they sought the shelter of distant and pathless wilds. Night and weariness of bloodshed put an end to the pursuit. About 10,000 of the enemy were slain, on our side there fell 360 men, and among them Aulus Atticus, the commander of the cohort, whose youthful impetuosity and mettlesome steed had borne him into the midst of the enemy. CHAP XXXVII

Scenes after the battle. Agricola's return southwards.

Elated by their victory and their booty, the conquerors passed a night of merriment, Meanwhile the Britons, wandering amidst the mingled wailings of men and women, were dragging off their wounded, calling to the unhurt, deserting their homes, and in their rage actually firing them, choosing places of concealment only instantly to abandon them. One moment they would take counsel together, the next, part company, while the sight of those who were dearest to them sometimes melted their hearts, but oftener roused their fury. It was an undoubted fact that some of them vented their rage on their wives and children, as if in pity for their lot. The following day showed more fully the extent of the calamity, for the silence of desolation reigned everywhere: the hills were forsaken, houses were smoking in the distance, and no one was seen by the scouts. These were despatched in all directions; and it having been ascertained that the track of the flying enemy was uncertain, and that there was no attempt at rallying, CHAP XXXVIII

CHAP. XXXVIII. it being also impossible, as summer was now over, to extend the war, Agricola led back his army into the territory of the Boresti. He received hostages from them, and then ordered the commander of the fleet to sail round Britain. A force for this purpose was given him, which great panic everywhere preceded. Agricola himself, leading his infantry and cavalry by slow marches, so as to overawe the newly-conquered tribes by the very tardiness of his progress, brought them into winter-quarters, while the fleet with propitious breezes and great renown entered the harbour of Trutulium, to which it had returned after having coasted along the entire southern shore of the island.

Domitian's vexation at the news of Agricola's success.

CHAP. XXXIX. Of this series of events, though not exaggerated in the despatches of Agricola by any boastfulness of language, Domitian heard, as was his wont, with joy in his face but anxiety in his heart. He felt conscious that all men laughed at his late mock triumph over Germany, for which there had been purchased from traders people whose dress and hair might be made to resemble those of captives, whereas now a real and splendid victory, with the destruction of thousands of the enemy, was being celebrated with just applause. It was, he thought, a very alarming thing for him that the name of a subject should be raised above that of the Emperor; it was to no purpose that he had driven into obscurity the pursuit of forensic eloquence and the graceful accomplishments of civil life, if another were to forestall the distinctions of war. To other glories he could more easily shut his eyes, but the greatness of a good general was a truly imperial quality. Harassed by these anxieties, and absorbed in an incommunicable trouble, a sure prognostic of some cruel purpose, he decided that it was best for the present to suspend his hatred until the freshness of Agricola's renown and his popularity with the army should begin to pass away. CHAP. XXXIX

Honours paid to Agricola His behaviour.

For Agricola was still the governor of Britain Accordingly the Emperor ordered that the usual triumphal decorations, the honour of a laurelled statue, and all that is commonly given in place of the triumphal procession, with the addition of many laudatory expressions, should be decreed in the senate, together with a hint to the effect that Agricola was to have the province of Syria, then vacant by the death of Atilius Rufus, a man of consular rank, and generally reserved for men of distinction. It was believed by many persons that one of the freedmen employed on confidential services was sent to Agricola, bearing a despatch in which Syria was offered him, and with instructions to deliver it should he be in Britain; that this freedman in crossing the straits met Agricola, and without even saluting him made his way back to Domitian; though I cannot say whether the story is true, or is only a fiction invented to suit the Emperor's character. CHAP. XL.

Meanwhile Agricola had handed over his province in peace and safety to his successor. And not to make his entrance into Rome conspicuous by the concourse of welcoming throngs, he avoided the

CHAP XL attentions of his friends by entering the city at night, and at night too, according to orders, proceeded to the palace, where, having been received with a hurried embrace and without a word being spoken, he mingled in the crowd of courtiers. Anxious henceforth to temper the military renown, which annoys men of peace, with other merits, he studiously cultivated retirement and leisure, simple in dress, courteous in conversation, and never accompanied but by one or two friends, so that the many who commonly judge of great men by their external grandeur, after having seen and attentively surveyed him, asked the secret of a greatness which but few could explain.

Agricola's danger.

CHAP XLI During this time he was frequently accused before Domitian in his absence, and in his absence acquitted The cause of his danger lay not in any crime, nor in any complaint of injury, but in a ruler who was the foe of virtue, in his own renown, and in that worst class of enemies—the men who praise. And then followed such days for the commonwealth as would not suffer Agricola to be forgotten; days when so many of our armies were lost in Mœsia, Dacia, Germany, and Pannonia, through the rashness or cowardice of our generals, when so many of our officers were besieged and captured with so many of our auxiliaries, when it was no longer the boundaries of empire and the banks of rivers which were imperilled, but the winter-quarters of our legions and the possession of our territories And so when disaster followed upon disaster, and the entire year was marked by destruction and slaughter, the voice of the people called Agricola to the command; for they all contrasted his vigour, firmness, and experience in war, with the inertness and timidity of other generals. This talk, it is quite certain, assailed the ears of the Emperor himself, while affection and loyalty in the best of his freedmen, malice and envy in the worst, kindled the anger of a prince ever inclined to evil And so at once, by his own excellences and by the faults of others, Agricola was hurried headlong to a perilous elevation. CHAP XLI

A.D. 90 *ÆT.* 52. *Agricola declines a pro-consulate.*

The year had now arrived in which the pro-consulate of Asia or Africa was to fall to him by lot, and, as Civica had been lately murdered, Agricola did not want a warning, or Domitian a precedent. Persons well acquainted with the Emperor's feelings came to ask Agricola, as if on their own account, whether he would go. First they hinted their purpose by praises of tranquillity and leisure; then offered their services in procuring acceptance for his excuses; and at last, throwing off all disguise, brought him by entreaties and threats to Domitian. The Emperor, armed beforehand with hypocrisy, and assuming a haughty demeanour, listened to his prayer that he might be excused, and having granted his request allowed himself to be formally thanked, nor blushed to grant so sinister a favour. But the salary usually granted to a pro-consul, and which he had himself given to some governors, he did not bestow on Agricola, either because he was offended at its not having been CHAP XLII

CHAP. XLII asked, or was warned by his conscience that he might be thought to have purchased the refusal which he had commanded. It is, indeed, human nature to hate the man whom you have injured; yet the Emperor, notwithstanding his irascible temper and an implacability proportioned to his reserve, was softened by the moderation and prudence of Agricola, who neither by a perverse obstinacy nor an idle parade of freedom challenged fame or provoked his fate. Let it be known to those whose habit it is to admire the disregard of authority, that there may be great men even under bad emperors, and that obedience and submission, when joined to activity and vigour, may attain a glory which most men reach only by a perilous career, utterly useless to the state, and closed by an ostentatious death.

A.D 93. *ÆT.* 55. *His death.*

CHAP. XLIII. The end of his life, a deplorable calamity to us and a grief to his friends, was regarded with concern even by strangers and those who knew him not. The common people and this busy population continually inquired at his house, and talked of him in public places and in private gatherings No man when he heard of Agricola's death could either be glad or at once forget it. Men's sympathy was increased by a prevalent rumour that he was destroyed by poison. For myself, I have nothing which I should venture to state for fact. Certainly during the whole of his illness the Emperor's chief freedmen and confidential physicians came more frequently than is usual with a court which pays its visits by means of messengers.

This was, perhaps, solicitude, perhaps espionage. Certain it is, that on the last day the very agonies of his dying moments were reported by a succession of couriers, and no one believed that there would be such haste about tidings which would be heard with regret. Yet in his manner and countenance the Emperor displayed some signs of sorrow, for he could now forget his enmity, and it was easier to conceal his joy than his fear. It was well known that on reading the will, in which he was named co-heir with Agricola's excellent wife and most dutiful daughter, he expressed delight, as if it had been a complimentary choice. So blinded and perverted was his mind by incessant flattery, that he did not know that it was only a bad Emperor whom a good father would make his heir. CHAP XLIII

His age. Remarks on him and on the circumstances of his death.

Agricola was born on the 13th of June, in the third consulate of Caius Cæsar; he died on the 23rd of August, during the consulate of Collega and Priscus, being in the fifty-sixth year of his age. Should posterity wish to know something of his appearance, it was graceful rather than commanding. There was nothing formidable in his appearance; a gracious look predominated. One would easily believe him a good man, and willingly believe him to be great. As for himself, though taken from us in the prime of a vigorous manhood, yet, as far as glory is concerned, his life was of the longest. Those true blessings, indeed, which consist in virtue, he had fully attained; and on one who had reached the honours of CHAP XLIV

CHAP. XLIV a consulate and a triumph, what more had fortune to bestow? Immense wealth had no attractions for him, and wealth he had, even to splendour. As his daughter and his wife survived him, it may be thought that he was even fortunate—fortunate, in that while his honours had suffered no eclipse, while his fame was at its height, while his kindred and his friends still prospered, he escaped from the evil to come. For, though to survive until the dawn of this most happy age and to see a Trajan on the throne was what he would speculate upon in previsions and wishes confided to my ears, yet he had this mighty compensation for his premature death, that he was spared those later years during which Domitian, leaving now no interval or breathing space of time, but, as it were, with one continuous blow, drained the life-blood of the Commonwealth.

CHAP. XLV Agricola did not see the senate-house besieged, or the senate hemmed in by armed men, or so many of our consulars falling at one single massacre, or so many of Rome's noblest ladies exiles and fugitives. Carus Metius had as yet the distinction of but one victory, and the noisy counsels of Messalinus were not heard beyond the walls of Alba, and Massa Bæbius was then answering for his life. It was not long before our hands dragged Helvidius to prison, before we gazed on the dying looks of Manricus and Rusticus, before we were steeped in Senecio's innocent blood. Even Nero turned his eyes away, and did not gaze upon the atrocities which he ordered; with Domitian it was the chief part of our miseries to see

CHAP XLV

and to be seen, to know that our sighs were being recorded, to have, ever ready to note the pallid looks of so many faces, that savage countenance reddened with the hue with which he defied shame.

Thou wast indeed fortunate, Agricola, not only in the splendour of thy life, but in the opportune moment of thy death. Thou submittedst to thy fate, so they tell us who were present to hear thy last words, with courage and cheerfulness, seeming to be doing all thou couldst to give thine Emperor full acquittal As for me and thy daughter, besides all the bitterness of a father's loss, it increases our sorrow that it was not permitted us to watch over thy failing health, to comfort thy weakness, to satisfy ourselves with those looks, those embraces. Assuredly we should have received some precepts, some utterances to fix in our inmost hearts. This is the bitterness of our sorrow, this the smart of our wound, that from the circumstance of so long an absence thou wast lost to us four years before. Doubtless, best of fathers, with that most loving wife at thy side, all the dues of affection were abundantly paid thee, yet with too few tears thou wast laid to thy rest, and in the light of thy last day there was something for which thine eyes longed in vain.

CHAP XLVI

If there is any dwelling-place for the spirits of the just; if, as the wise believe, noble souls do not perish with the body, rest thou in peace; and call us, thy family, from weak regrets and womanish laments to the contemplation of thy virtues, for which we must not weep nor beat the breast. Let us honour thee

CHAP. XLVI.

not so much with transitory praises as with our reverence, and, if our powers permit us, with our emulation. That will be true respect, that the true affection of thy nearest kin. This, too, is what I would enjoin on daughter and wife, to honour the memory of that father, that husband, by pondering in their hearts all his words and acts, by cherishing the features and lineaments of his character rather than those of his person, It is not that I would forbid the likenesses which are wrought in marble or in bronze ; but as the faces of men, so all similitudes of the face are weak and perishable things, while the fashion of the soul is everlasting, such as may be expressed not in some foreign substance, or by the help of art, but in our own lives. Whatever we loved, whatever we admired in Agricola, survives, and will survive in the hearts of men, in the succession of the ages, in the fame that waits on noble deeds. Over many indeed, of those who have gone before, as over the inglorious and ignoble, the waves of oblivion will roll ; Agricola, made known to posterity by history and tradition, will live for ever.

NOTES ON THE

LIFE OF AGRICOLA.

(1) *Many too thought that to write their own lives showed the confidence of integrity rather than presumption. (Ac plerique, suam ipsi vitam narrare, fiduciam potius morum, quam arrogantiam arbitrati sunt.)*

"Fiducia morum" seems naturally to mean "the confidence inspired by a good character." The word "fiducia" usually denotes "a well-grounded, and therefore praiseworthy, trust" in anything. Possibly by "morum" may be meant the manners of *the* age in which Rutilius and Scaurus lived. To write their own lives was, in fact, to bear a testimony to the virtues of a less corrupt time; and they would feel that to praise themselves was, in fact, to praise the State. But the difference between these two meanings is very slight. CHAP. I

Of Rutilius and Scaurus no one doubted the honesty or questioned the motives

Rutilius, who was consul 105 B C., is spoken of by Cicero (De Orat. i. 53) as a man of learning, devoted to philosophy, and of singular virtue and integrity.

CHAP. I In the Brutus (ch. 29), he is named with Scaurus; both are said to have been experienced, though not first-rate orators, men of great industry and some talent, but not possessed of true oratorical genius. Rutilius was a Stoic, and a pupil of Panætius. He wrote a history of Rome in Greek, which is referred to by Livy (xxxix. 52). His memoir of himself and of his times is mentioned only by Tacitus. Rutilius Rufus and Aurelius Scaurus were contemporaries and rivals. Each impeached the other for bribery, in seeking to obtain the consulate. Scaurus was "princeps Senatus," and twice consul, in 115 B.C. and 107 B.C.

Tacitus here refers to Scaurus's autobiography in three books, of which Cicero says (Brutus, 29) that it was good enough (*sane utiles*), but that it was read by no one. He began life as a poor man, though by birth a patrician, and succeeded in raising his family to the highest distinction.

But in these days I who have to record the life of one who has passed away must crave an indulgence, which I should not have had to ask had I only to inveigh against an age so cruel, so hostile to all virtue. (*At nunc narraturo mihi vitam defuncti hominis, venia opus fuit; quam non petissem, incusaturus tam sæva et infesta virtutibus tempora.*)

We take Tacitus's meaning to be this:—"I should not have thought it necessary to offer any apology for my work, were that work to be merely a satire on a bad age, and not also the praise of a good man." A very similar sentiment occurs Hist. ii. 1:—"From a writer's adulation we should instinctively shrink, while we lend a ready ear to detraction and spite." So here Tacitus implies that invective and satire would be sure to be popular, and would, therefore, need no apology. There is another meaning which the passage may bear; it is this:—"Under any other circumstances I should not have apologized for this biography, since in writing it I am necessarily about to censure a bad age." Ritter reads "incursaturus" for "incusaturus," because he thinks that the meaning of "incusaturus" is obscure, and the idea conveyed not suited to the better time of Trajan in which Tacitus was writing Accordingly, he explains the passage thus:—"I should not have thought of offering an apology had I been writing in Domitian's reign, and thereby likely to offend one who hated virtue; such an apology would have been an insult to the Emperor." But is not this explanation of the passage as far-fetched as that to which he objects? "Incusaturus," it should be observed, is the reading of the MSS. Orelli and Wex retain it. CHAP I

We have read that the panegyrics pronounced by Arulenus Rusticus on Pætus Thrasea and by Herennius Senecio on Priscus Helvidius were made capital crimes. (Legimus, cum Aruleno Rustico Pætus Thrasea, Herennio Senecioni Priscus Helvidius laudati essent, capitale fuisse)

Tacitus had probably read an account of these horrors during his absence from Rome, in letters from his own personal friends, and possibly in memoirs and CHAP II

CHAP. II panegyrics composed by some of the senators in honour of the men here mentioned. He can hardly be referring to the "Acta Diurna," for Domitian, so we learn from Dion Cassius, would not allow the memory of his victims to be recorded.

Arulenus Rusticus, or, as his full name seems to have been, L. Arulenus Junius Rusticus, was a Stoic, and an intimate friend of Pætus Thrasea, whom, as a tribune of the plebs, A D. 66, in Nero's reign, he would have interposed to save by means of his tribunitial "veto" had Thrasea permitted him. Suetonius (Domit x) says he was put to death by Domitian for having written panegyrics on Thrasea and Helvidius Priscus, in which he spoke of them as "sanctissimi viri" Tacitus, however, is probably right in attributing the latter panegyric to Herennius Senecio, and his testimony is confirmed by Pliny (i. 5, 14; iii. 11). Senecio was put to death on the accusation of Caius Metius, and his chief crime seems to have been this laudatory memoir of Helvidius Priscus.

Arulenus Rusticus and Herennius Senecio are again mentioned, ch. 45; and Mauricus, a brother of the former is also named in the same passage. He was one of Pliny's intimate friends, who says of him (iv 22), "Quo viro nihil firmius, nihil verius." This character of him is well illustrated in the Hist. iv. 40, where we are told that on the first day on which Domitian took his seat in the Senate, Mauricus asked him to give the Senators access to the Imperial registers with the view of ascertaining what impeachments the several informers had proposed, and thereby calling them to account.

The conscience of mankind (conscientiam humani generis). CHAP. II

We have ventured to render "conscientia" by "conscience," although of course the precise meaning is, "the knowledge which all men had of the virtues of those who have been above named." In this, the idea of approval is implied, so that "conscientia" may be fairly taken to express, "the faculty which approves." The word has acquired almost the exact meaning of our "conscience" in Tacitus and the writers of the Silver Age. It occurs three times in the Agricola, in ch. i. ii. and xlii., in all which passages it seems to be adequately represented by its English derivative.

Nerva Trajanus.

Trajan was so called after his adoption by Nerva. CHAP. III

The public safety (securitas publica).

The force of the original (which can hardly be reproduced in a translation) turns on the fact that "public safety" (*securitas publica*) was personified as a kind of goddess, and represented on coins of the Antonine periods under the figure of a woman, in a sitting posture, with her right hand on her head.

Those fifteen years.

Domitian reigned from 81 A.D. to 96 A.D.

The beauty and splendour (pulchritudinem ac speciem).

Perhaps the word "species" is used in its philo- CHAP. IV
sophical sense, and denotes the ἰδέα of Plato. The

CHAP. IV. context rather favours this view. The expression would thus mean "the highest imaginable glory." Tacitus, it should be observed, likes occasionally to use philosophical language.

He retained from his learning that most difficult of lessons, moderation. (Retinuitque, quod est difficillimum, ex sapientia modum.)

"Modum" must mean "moderation," "self-control," what the Greeks expressed by σωφροσύνη, or perhaps "the due mean in all things," the τὸ μέσον of Aristotle. The lesson which Agricola retained from his philosophical studies was to avoid excess in any direction, and Tacitus no doubt implies a favourable contrast between him and some of the more extreme Stoics with whom he was acquainted.

Salvius Titianus.

CHAP. VI. He was the elder brother of the Emperor Otho.

However, the good wife deserves the greater praise, just as the bad incurs a heavier censure. (Nisi quod in bona uxore tanto major laus, quanto in mala plus culpæ est.)

This sentence is not quite clearly expressed, but the idea is, that the virtues of a good wife are esteemed more highly by the world than those of a good husband, just as the faults of a bad wife are more severely censured than those of a bad husband. We often hear it said that a bad woman is worse than a bad man.

The son that had before been born to him. (*Filium ante sublatum*) CHAP VI

The original would be more nearly represented by the term "acknowledged." A Roman father took up (*sustulit*) the new-born child, thus acknowledging him as his own, and declaring that he was to be reared. Children born in excess of a certain number, *post constitutam familiam* or *agnati*, to use Roman phrases, were not reared. Compare Hist. v. 5, Germania, 19.

The usual judicial functions did not fall to his lot. (*Nec enim jurisdictio obvenerat*)

Agricola was neither "prætor urbanus" nor "prætor peregrinus," and Tacitus tells us (Ann. iv. 6) that all cases in which the State was involved, and even all the more important private cases, were disposed of by the Senate, so that his prætorship must have been a sinecure.

The games and the pageantry of his office he ordered according to the mean between strictness and profusion, avoiding extravagance but not missing distinction. (*Ludos et inania honoris medio rationis atque abundantiæ duxit, uti longe à luxuria, ita famæ propior*)

The general meaning of this passage is sufficiently obvious, but we cannot believe that we have exactly what Tacitus wrote. Whatever reading be adopted, there is extreme difficulty about the word "duxit," to which it seems hardly possible to give any tolerable sense. It can scarcely be equivalent to "edidit," for, as Ernesti pointed out, there is no authority for such an expression as "ducere ludos." It is possible that

CHAP VI "duxit ludos" may mean "he managed, or regulated the games," and that the idea of the whole sentence is something of this kind: "He guided, or made them pass through the mean between strictness and profusion" Ritter adopts the conjecture of Lipsius, and for "medio rationis" reads "moderationis," and he thinks the sense is: "He considered that the games required for their due celebration a moderate yet, at the same time, a sufficiently ample expenditure" It seems very doubtful whether this meaning can be fairly extracted from the words. For the present, we think we may as well read with Orelli, "medio rationis," which, at all events, has MSS. authority, though we admit we are not satisfied with it.

The late prætorian officer (nec legatus prætorius).

CHAP VII This was Roscius Cælius, of whom we are told, Hist i. 60, that he was on bad terms with the Governor of Britain, Trebellius Maximus, whom he insulted, and actually drove from the province. His audacity, it is here said, gave him the chief influence with the soldiery; here it seems to be implied that he was, perhaps, too weak to control them. The meaning, however, is that either his own seditious temper or that of the soldiers was in fault. As an officer, too, of merely prætorian rank he would carry less weight than a consular commander.

He was altogether without harshness, pride, or the greed of gain. (Tristitiam et arrogantiam et avaritiam exuerat)

CHAP IX It has been said that "avaritia" cannot have its usual meaning in this passage, because it could not be

well joined with "tristitia" and "arrogantia," which CHAP IX
denote qualities so widely different, and because, too, we are told immediately afterwards that to speak of purity and integrity in such a man would be an insult to his virtues Orelli therefore thinks that by "avaritia" is meant extreme sternness and severity in the collection of the revenues[1] It has been explained by some to be excessive parsimony and shabbiness in all money matters. But "avaritia" always seems to have a much stronger meaning than this, and to express an "eager grasping after more." So in this passage we have rendered it the "greed of gain." There might be the anxiety to amass a fortune without anything like actual dishonesty, or, indeed, anything incompatible with the virtues expressed by "integritas" and "abstinentia." And a man, in this sense "avarus," might be also "tristis" and "arrogans."

Many writers (multis scriptoribus).

The reference is to Cæsar, Pliny, Ptolemy, Dio- CHAP X
dorus Siculus, Strabo, Fabius Rusticus, Mela.

So that it has become the popular description of the whole island. (Unde et in universum fama est transgressa)

Kritz reads "transgressis" for "transgressa," and explains the passage to mean that those who had crossed over from the continent gave the description of Britain just mentioned to the whole island, *i.e.* to

[1] Galba is said to have been "publice avarus."

CHAP. X. Britain with Caledonia. "Transgressis" certainly has the authority of one MS., but "transgressa" has the merit of being a clear and intelligible reading, which can hardly be said for the other. Indeed it seems barely possible to get from it the meaning given by Kritz.

Which as yet had been hidden by the snows of winter. (Quam hactenus nix et hiems abdebat.)

We have translated the conjectural reading "quam hactenus nix et hiems abdebat," as perhaps, on the whole, the best, where none are by any means satisfactory. The passage seems too corrupt to admit of certain emendation.

Thule can hardly be Iceland. It is more probably Mainland, the largest of the Shetland Isles.

The dependants fight (propugnant).

CHAP. XII. The word may mean "fight from the chariot," or merely "fight for him," *i.e.* "do the fighting." The Germans thus reversed, in this case, the practice with which the readers of the Iliad are familiar.

This Augustus spoke of as policy, Tiberius as an inherited maxim. (Consilium id divus Augustus vocabat, Tiberius præceptum.)

CHAP. XIII. A passage in Ann. i. 11 explains this. Augustus added to the Imperial register, written by his own hand, and containing a summary of the resources of the empire, a recommendation that certain fixed limits and boundaries should be observed. Tiberius always professed the greatest respect for everything said or done by the father who had adopted him. In Ann. iv. 37 he is represented as saying that he looked on all the deeds and words of Augustus as law.

But his purposes, rapidly formed, were easily changed. (*Ni velox ingenio, mobilis pœnitentiæ.*)

Here we have translated from Orelli. Kritz reads "mobili" for "mobilis," and construes "velox" with "pœnitentiæ," which he takes as a genitive, and would render the words thus: "swift to repent, because of his fickle temper." But the passage to which he refers us (Ann. vi. 45), "commotus ingenio" (which expression is also used of Caligula), does not convince us that he is right. His reading perhaps makes the construction a little neater; still we do not see why "mobilis pœnitentiæ" is not a legitimate expression.

The first to renew the attempt. (*Auctor iterati operis*)

Nothing can be made out of the reading of the MSS., "auctoritate operis," which Orelli leaves as he finds. We have adopted what we look on as the almost certain emendation of Wex and Doderlin ("auctor iterati operis"), which Kritz approves By "opus" is to be understood the laborious and difficult operation of invading and conquering Britain, which Julius Cæsar was the first, and Claudius the second, to attempt. "Auctor," though usually applied to one who begins a work, means also one who completes it.

CHAP. XIII. *Destiny learnt to know its favourite (monstratus fatis Vespasianus).*

"Fatis" must, we think, be the dative. If it were the ablative, the preposition "a" seems wanted. The meaning would then be, "Vespasian was marked out by destiny." Ernesti, and after him Orelli, explain the passage to mean that he was "pointed out to," and, so to speak, commended to destiny and fortune as one worthy of empire. We think they are right.

A colony of veterans was also introduced. (Addita insuper veteranorum colonia.)

CHAP. XIV. Tacitus means Camalodunum (Colchester). "Camalus" answered to Mars, hence "Camalodunum," the city of Mars.

Of having enlarged the sphere of government (fama aucti officii.)

The "officium" of a governor would be to maintain the boundaries of his province; if he enlarged them, he might be said "augere officium." This appears to be the meaning of the expression.

The centurions of the one, the slaves of the other, combine violence with insult. (Alterius manus centuriones alterius servos vim et contumeliam miscere.)

CHAP. XV. There is here some confusion in the MSS., and one is obliged to have recourse to conjecture. Orelli, following Od. Muller, reads "alterius manus centuriones, alterius servos;" and explains it thus, "the instruments of the one, i.e. the legate, are his centurions." He illustrates this use of "manus" from Cic.

Verr. ii. 18, 27: "Comites illi tui delecti *manus* erant tuæ." But the construction is awkward, and the word "esse" seems to be absolutely required, to answer to "miscere" We have here followed Ritter. who omits "manus," which he thinks found its way into the text by way of an attempted correction. The MSS. generally have "centurionis," and it was this genitive which he supposes caused perplexity. Ritter's conjecture is perhaps as good as any, where all are very doubtful. CHAP XV

Excellent as he was in other respects. (*Ni, quamquam egregius cetera*, &c)

We have followed Orelli and Wex, who read "ni" Kritz reads "ne," as being closer to the MSS., which have "nequaquam." This, of course, entirely alters the meaning of the passage, and makes it point to the apprehensions of the Britons, instead of being the historian's assertion as a matter of fact But the words "quamquam egregius cetera," which must, we think, be meant to express Tacitus's own view of Paullinus, seem to be in this case very awkwardly interposed. We therefore prefer "ni" to "ne." CHAP XVI

Trebellius, who never ventured on a campaign (*nullis castrorum experimentis.*)

The meaning is that Trebellius was only a carpet soldier. The ablative "nullis experimentis" describes his character; he had had no actual experience of war.

When however Vespasian had restored to unity Britain as well as the rest of the world. (Sed ubi cum cetero orbe et Britanniam recuperavit.)

CHAP. XVII. As Vespasian cannot well be said to have "recovered" or "reconquered" the world, we have rendered the word "recuperavit," "restored to unity." The Empire had been distracted by civil war; Vespasian's accession to power restored peace and unity. What was lost was in this sense recovered Possibly too there may be latent in the word "recuperavit" the idea that Vespasian was eminently worthy of empire.

Any other successor (Alterius successoris.)

Kritz understands by "alterius" not *Frontinus* the immediate successor of Cerialis, but Agricola, the successor of Montinus. Is not this over subtle? We suppose he will not allow "alter" to have the sense of "different." But has it not this sense, Hist. ii. 90, "tamquam apud *alterius* civitatis senatum"? Besides it is extremely improbable that Tacitus would even suggest a comparison between Cerialis and the great man whose life he was writing.

Moved him in the selection of centurions and soldiers. (Milites ascire.)

CHAP. XIX. The MSS. (which Orelli follows) have "nescire," from which it seems impossible to extract any tolerable meaning We think "ascire" (which Wex and Kritz read) an almost certain emendation. The allusion is to what was called the "cohors prætoris," which is continually mentioned by Cicero in his speeches, and which was made up of lictors, secretaries, criers, and various attendants on the governor of a province They were commonly selected from the soldiers, and, as they were exempted from all purely military duties, they were called "beneficiarii." CHAP XIX

Hitherto the people had been compelled to endure the farce of waiting by the closed granary and of purchasing corn unnecessarily and raising it to a fictitious price. (*Namque per ludibrium assidere clausis horreis et emere ultro frumenta ac ludere pretio cogebantur.*)

There is some difficulty about "ludere pretio," to which, as appearing in the MSS, Orelli adheres Ritter substitutes for "ludere" the rare word "colludere," which is found in the sense of "to be in collusion with," and is so used by Cicero (Verr. ii. 2, 24) It would no doubt suit this passage very well. But it is quite conceivable that Tacitus might use "ludere" in the same sense. He often prefers simple words to compound. The force of the word turns on the fact that the whole affair was a kind of jest and mockery; they were bidding one against another without any real necessity, and thus absurdly raising the price. It was not a *bonâ fide* transaction; it was a species of mock auction. "Ludere pretio" must be a similar phrase to "ludere aleâ." By the "closed granaries" we understand the public granaries, which would be under the control of the governer. The "publicani" would buy up all the corn of the country and store it in these granaries, so that the

CHAP. XIX. farmers would be obliged to buy it back on whatever terms they could, and the price would be greatly enhanced by their competition. Cicero charges Verres with having oppressed his province in this among many other ways. Wex's emendation of "luere," which he explains by "luere imperata" (to discharge was required of them), is ingenious, but seems unnecessary. Kritz conjectures "recludere" in the sense of "to close again." We doubt whether the word will bear this meaning.

But the Britons, thinking themselves baffled, &c. (*At Britanni . . . . . rati*)

CHAP. XXVII. Here we have adopted the conjecture of Kritz, who supplies "clusos" before "rati" a word which Tacitus elsewhere uses absolutely. Wex and Orelli think there is a more considerable *lacuna* in the passage.

The same summer a Usipian cohort, which had been levied in Germany and transported into Britain, ventured on a great and memorable exploit. (*Eâdem æstate cohors Usipiorum, per Germanias conscripta et in Britanniam transmissa, magnum et memorabile facinus ausa est*)

CHAP. XXVIII. The Usipii are mentioned (Germ 32) with the Tencteri, as dwellers on the Rhine. (See Sketch of the Geography of the Germania) This Usipian cohort, levied in Germany (*per Germanias*, that is, the Roman provinces of Upper and Lower Germany), belonged probably to the troops which Agricola, in his fifth campaign, had posted in that part of Britain which looks towards Ireland (ch. 24), and which consequently, would be in the neighbourhood of the Frith of Clyde. The "memorable exploit on which they ventured" is mentioned also by Dion, who tells us (lxvi. 20) that, having mutinied, they put out to sea, sailed round the western parts of Britain, as the wind and waves carried them, and eventually reached Agricola's camp on the other side of the island. This account is certainly less vague than that of Tacitus, and it would seem to imply that they sailed from the Frith of Clyde round the north of Scotland and then down the eastern coast to the Frith of Forth. Once in the German Ocean, it is perfectly conceivable that they might have been carried to some point on the German coast, near the mouth of the Weser or the Elbe Had they sailed southwards round Cornwall, and entered the British Channel, as some have supposed, it is difficult to see how this could have happened. Tacitus and Dion cannot well be reconciled except on the supposition that they sailed round Scotland. Dr. Merivale thinks that all they did was to run down the east coast from the Forth till they came opposite Friesland. In fact, he rejects Dion's account. (See "Hist. of Romans under the Empire," ch. lxi)

Dispersing in search of water. (*Mox ad aquam,* &c)

This is one of those passages from which no meaning can be extracted, except by very hazardous conjecture. Orelli leaves it.

CHAP. XXX. *This remote sanctuary of Britain's glory has up to this time been a defence.* (*Recessus ipse ac sinus famæ in hunc diem defendit.*)

We think it far better to take "famæ" as the genitive depending on "sinus" than, with Orelli, as a dative governed by "defendit." He compares such passages as Virg. Ec. vii. 47, "Solstitium pecori defendite," and Hor. Car. i. 17, 3, "Defendit æstatem capellis;" and he renders the passage thus: "the very remoteness of our situation protects us from fame," *i.e.* as yet we are all but unknown. This seems obscure and far-fetched, and though no doubt "sinus famæ" is a bold expression, still we think Tacitus may have used it to denote "the last and most remote retreat of glory;" or he may possibly have wished to convey the notion that fame, like a tutelary goddess, was folding the Caledonians to her bosom. Ritter takes this last view.

Never likely to abuse our freedom (*libertatem non in pœnitentiam laturi*).

CHAP. XXXI. It is not easy to give the force of these words, or indeed to construe them. The meaning seems to be, "We are not likely to bear our freedom so as afterwards to have cause for sorrow that we have been free." The Brigantes had been spoilt by success, or they would have recovered their freedom. Galgacus implies that success will not have the same bad effect on his people, but that they will use their freedom better, and hold it fast.

The towns are ill-affected. (*Ægra municipia*)

Wex and Kritz read "mancipia" for "municipia" Wex says that there are two objections to "municipia;" (1) We know only of one "municipium" in Britain, Verulamium; (2) "ægra" would not mean "wavering" or "disloyal," but disturbed by internal faction. But is not the passage clearly rhetorical, and may it not be compared with the "incensæ coloniæ" in ch. v.? Strictly speaking, we know only of one "colonia," Camalodunum. It is quite possible that Camalodunum, Verulamium, and Londinium may be loosely described under the term "municipia." As to the word "æger," it seems rash to pronounce that its original meaning "feeble," "unsound," may not be transferred to the idea of "doubtful loyalty," as much as to that of "internal discord." We see no great force in Wex's remark that, if Galgacus had meant to speak of the doubtful attitude of the "municipia" towards the Romans, he would have rather chosen a word which expressed the recovery of health. Relatively to the *Romans*, the municipia were in an unhealthy state (*ægra*). In our translation we have, for the above reasons, adhered to Orelli's reading, *municipia*. CHAP XXXII.

All that is commonly given in place of the triumphal procession (*quidquid pro triumpho datur*).

By this seems to be meant what was called the "supplicatio," a formal thanksgiving to the gods when a great victory had been gained. It took place before the triumphal procession (*triumphus*), but was not always followed by it. CHAP. XL.

He studiously cultivated retirement and leisure. (*Tranquillitatem atque otium penitus auxit.*

CHAP. XI. We doubt whether "auxit" (the established reading) will bear the meaning which we have given to it, or, indeed, any meaning. Wex conjectures "hausit" (drank deep of)

During this time he was frequently accused before Domitian in his absence. (*Crebro per eos dies apud Domitianum absens accusatus.*)

CHAP. XLI. Agricola had for enemies such men as M Regulus, Veiento, Publius Certus, all notorious "delatores"

An ostentatious death (*ambitiosâ morte*).

CHAP. XLII. "Ambitiosa mors" is a death by which a man seeks glory The word "ambitiosus" comes very near to our "ostentatious."

For he could now forget his enmity (*securus jam odii*).

CHAP. XLIII. We observe that Dr. Merivale, in a paraphrase of this passage in chap. lxii. of his "History of the Romans under the Empire," takes these words in the sense of "though reckless by this time of popular hatred" But we think it more probable that by "odium" is meant Domitian's hatred of Agricola, and that it is better and simpler to take "securus odii" as an explanation of the reason why he now showed his sorrow. This was the view of Lipsius, and it is approved by Orelli. So too Louandre: "Tranquille désormais sur l'objet de sa haine"

The walls of Alba (*Albanam arcem*).

By "arx Albana" Tacitus means a favourite country-house of Domitian's at the foot of the "Mons Albanus," and seventeen miles from Rome. Here he would receive information, and occasionally even summon a meeting of the Senate. Juvenal designates it by the same term (Sat. iv. 145):—

> "Misso proceres exire jubentur,
> Consilio quos Albanam dux magnus in arcem
> Traxerat"

Suetonius (Domitian, iv) says that here too the Emperor celebrated every year the festival of Minerva.

Carus Metius was one of the most notorious of the "delatores" in the time of Domitian. He is named by Juvenal (i. 36), by Martial (xii. 25), and by Pliny, who (Epist. vii. 19) says that there was found in the Emperor's desk after his death an information against himself

Messalinus. This was the infamous Catullus Messalinus, whom Juvenal (iv. 115) thus describes:—

> "Grande et conspicuum nostro quoque tempore monstrum"

He was blind, and Pliny (Epist. iv. 22) tells us that "to a savage temper he added all the evil qualities which sometimes accompany blindness, he knew neither fear, or shame, or pity, and the Emperor would make use of him, as one might throw a weapon at random, for the destruction of all the best citizens." He is probably the man who, according to Josephus (Bell. Jud. vii. 11), was governor of the Libyan Pentapolis in the reigns of Vespasian and Titus, and

CHAP. XLV.

there contrived to involve a number of Jewish provincials, and Josephus among them, in a false charge of treason.

Massa Bæbius. Massa Bæbius is mentioned in the Hist. (iv. 50) as one of the procurators of Africa, "a name even then fatal to the good, and destined often to reappear among the causes of the sufferings which we had ere long to endure." The reference in the present passage is to his impeachment by the province of Bætica, which, as governor, he had plundered and oppressed. The younger Pliny and Herennius Senecio defended the provincials. Bæbius was condemned.

Helvidius. Helvidius was an intimate friend of the younger Pliny. He was one of Domitian's many victims. Pliny tells us (Epist. ix. 13) that after the Emperor's death he made up his mind to avenge the murder of his friend by impeaching the man who had been his bitterest accuser, one Publicius Certus, a senator of prætorian rank. Helvidius was the son of the Helvidius Priscus whom Tacitus praises so warmly (Hist. iv. 5), who was the son-in-law of Pætus Thrasea, and who owed his death under Vespasian to his courageous freedom of speech. The charge against him, as we learn from Suetonius (Domit. x.), was that in a comic piece which he had composed under the title of "Paris and Œnone," he had really ridiculed the Emperor's divorce from one of his wives. With an obsequious Senate such a charge proved fatal to him. Tacitus says "*our* hands," because he was himself a senator, though it is doubtful whether he was at Rome at the time.

Mauricus, Rusticus, Senecio. See notes on ch. ii. CHAP XLV

That savage countenance, reddened with the hue with which he defied shame (*sævus ille vultus et rubor quo se contra pudorem muniebat*).

A passage in the Hist. (iv. 40) illustrates the word "rubor." We are told that on the occasion of Domitian's taking his seat in the Senate and making his first speech, "the frequent blush on his countenance passed for modesty." Suetonius (Domit. xviii.), in describing his appearance, mentions "a redness of face" as one of his natural peculiarities.

With transitory praises (*temporalibus laudibus*).

Ritter, following Lipsius, reads "immortalibus" for the rare word "temporalibus" which is found in the MSS. We cannot see that anything is thus gained; indeed we think that the context is rather in favour of "temporalibus" in the sense of "feeble, transitory." The meaning appears to be: "Feeble though we are, let us do our best to honour Agricola with such praises and such imitation as our powers permit." The epithet "immortalis" would not suit this meaning. Tacitus is not speaking of this particular memoir, but of the every-day praises which Agricola's family would bestow on him. CHAP XLVI

GERMANY AND ITS TRIBES.

London & Cambridge: Macmillan & Co.

INTRODUCTION TO THE GERMANY.

THE following passage of the Germany[1] enables us to fix the date of its composition. "Rome was in her 640th year when we first heard of the Cimbrian invader in the consulship of Cæcilius Metellus and Papirius Carbo, from which time to the second consulship of the Emperor Trajan we find to be an interval of about 210 years." It must, therefore, have been written A.U C. 851, A.D. 98.

Various, some of them extravagantly wild, conjectures have been hazarded as to the purpose of the work. It would tax our ingenuity to imagine a more improbable supposition than that Tacitus deliberately intended to furnish Trajan with information about the character and situation of the different Germanic tribes, with a view to the invasion and possible conquest of the country. The Emperor, we have little doubt, knew quite as much about Germany as the historian, and, had he known less, it is difficult to see how the vague and imperfect descriptions of the work in question could have helped him in planning a cam-

[1] Germany, chap 37.

paign Of this Tacitus must have been well aware. A much more plausible notion, and one which has found favour with several editors and translators, is, that in the rude and simple virtues of the Germans Tacitus saw a conspicuous contrast to Roman degeneracy, as well as the germs of future greatness. We think there is probably some truth in this view, though we cannot give it our unqualified assent There are certainly passages in the Germany which suggest a comparison between the merits of barbarian simplicity and the complicated evils of a highly artificial and luxurious civilization. But while Tacitus dwells on the virtues of the Germans, he shows that he was by no means insensible to their weaknesses and vices. He particularly mentions their extreme addiction to drunkenness and gambling. While he recognises in them a formidable foe to the Empire, and is prompted in one place[1] to speak of them with an almost savage hatred, he still seems to have thought meanly of their capacity for united action. We see no reason for believing that he anticipated fatal disasters to Rome from the side of Germany, or that he dimly perceived the signs of a new world in the many noble qualities of its free and brave peoples. Tacitus was a thorough and genuine Roman, though he feared and hated the corruptions of his age, and perhaps felt with satisfaction that his work was an indirect satire on them, yet he appears to have had great confidence in the destinies of Rome—a confidence which was, no doubt, strengthened by the outward splendour and prosperity of Trajan's reign.

[1] Germany, chap 33

If we are to indulge in conjecture, we should say that the passage[1] in which he enumerates the Roman losses in Germany explains the historian's motive. His imagination was evidently impressed by the combined phenomena of a multitude of fierce independent tribes, and of an indefinite tract of country, "bristling," as he describes it, "with forests, or reeking with swamps." The apparent impossibility of ever bringing it within the limits of the Empire, and the vaguely terrible stories which were certain to be current at Rome about the horrors of the climate and the strange aspect and ferocious barbarism of the inhabitants, would be certain to invest the subject with interest for Roman readers.

Ritter[2] has somewhat ingeniously, and not unreasonably, suggested that Tacitus intended the Germany to be a kind of explanatory appendix to the History, in which he has frequently occasion to describe campaigns of which that country was the scene There is nothing in this notion which necessarily clashes with the hints which we have just thrown out. It derives, perhaps, some support from the fact that the Germany is the only work of Tacitus which has no kind of preface We attach little importance to Ritter's remark that it may be compared to the sketch[3] of the origin and manners of the Jews, only that, from its greater length, it could not have conveniently found a place in the History. We are by no means convinced that it was not designed to be a

[1] Germany, chap 37.
[2] Ritter, Tacit. Proemium, 9.
[3] See Hist. v. 2 –13

distinct and complete work in itself, and we think it at least probable that some intimation would have been given of the character and purpose which Ritter assigns to it.

Another question which can be answered only by conjecture is, "What were Tacitus's sources of information respecting Germany? Was he personally acquainted with the country, or did he rely solely on the accounts of others?" On this point we have no evidence whatever; we are dependent wholly on what can be inferred from his works. Kritz, in the preface to his edition of the Germany, published in 1860, argues very confidently, from certain passages, that Tacitus had visited the country. He notices the use of German words, such as *framea* (spear), *glesum* (amber), as implying some knowledge of the language. He thinks that some of the descriptions—those, for instance, of the houses and of the cattle—seem to come from an eye-witness; and that here and there an expression indicates that the writer's information was drawn from the natives. But we cannot see why all this may not be accounted for by supposing that Tacitus had often conversed with Roman officers who had served in Germany. He must have had many opportunities of learning all that he has told us about the country and its people. The elder Pliny, who knew it personally from military service, had described in twenty books, now lost, the Germanic wars, a work which, from its length, may be supposed to have treated the subject exhaustively. Whether Tacitus, as has been thought, passed those last four years of Agricola's life (A.D. 89 to 93), of which he speaks with such sadness,[1] in Germany, must be matter of pure conjecture.

The Germany presents a number of difficult geographical and ethnological questions. The latter we have not attempted to discuss For the geography, which Tacitus very imperfectly defines, we have consulted, among others, Dr. Latham's edition, which is full of curious and interesting matter. The map exhibits only those tribes which are mentioned in the work. In the Annals and History there occur several names[2] which are not found in the Germany. The omission was not, as far as we can see, intentional. It was due, probably, to the incompleteness of the historian's knowledge.

It is to be observed that, by Germany, Tacitus means what the Romans spoke of as "Germany beyond the Rhine," as distinguished from the provinces of Upper and Lower Germany on the west bank of the river.

[1] Life of Agricola, chap 45.
[2] The Sugambri, Gugerni, Ampsivarii, Tubantes, Canninefates.

GEOGRAPHICAL NOTES TO THE GERMANY.

THE Germany of Tacitus is, as we should expect, an ill-defined geographical area. The Rhine and Danube are its western and southern boundaries. The Rhine divided it from Gaul, the Danube from Vindelicia, Noricum, and Pannonia. Its eastern boundary, which parted it from Dacia and Sarmatia, is vaguely described as "mutuus metus aut montes" (ch. 1). Approximately, however, we may say that a point in the Danube a little above Pesth, where the river makes a sharp bend, is its south-eastern corner. If from this point we draw a straight line to Cracow, and then follow the course of the Vistula, we shall get what nearly represents the eastern boundary. Tacitus certainly mentions tribes which must have been to the east of the Vistula, but he intimates that it is doubtful whether they were, for the most part, properly German. Northwards lay the imperfectly known regions of the Baltic, which he speaks of as "broad promontories and vast islands" (ch. 1). All this he includes in Germany, which he therefore conceived as comprehending Scandinavia, and as having no known boundary on the north. For the assistance of our readers, we have given in the following table the modern localities of the various tribes which he mentions. This of course cannot be done with absolute precision.

We have thought it unnecessary that all these tribes should appear in the map.

Æstii (chap 45)—The *Æstii* occupied that part of Prussia which is to the north-east of the Vistula. Their northern boundary was the Baltic ("Suevicum Mare"). The name still survives in the form "Estonia."

Angli (chap. 40).—The *Angli* were a Suevic clan. They occupied, probably, the larger part of Sleswick-Holstein, and, possibly, the northern districts of Hanover.

Angrivarii (chap. 33).—The settlements of the Angrivarii were to the west of the Weser (Visurgis), in the neighbourhood of Minden and Herford, and thus coincide, to some extent, with Westphalia. Their territory was the scene of Varus' defeat. It has been thought that the name of this tribe is preserved in that of the town Engern.

Aravisci (chap. 28)—The locality of the Aravisci was the extreme north-eastern part of the province of Pannonia, and would thus stretch from Vienna (Vindobona) eastwards to Raab (Arrabo), taking in a portion of the south-west of Hungary.

Aviones (chap. 40).—The Aviones were a Suevic clan. They are mentioned by Tacitus in connexion with the Reudigni, Angli, Varini, Eudoses, Suardones, and Nuithones, all Suevic clans. These tribes must have occupied Mecklenburg-Schwerin, Mecklenburg-Strelitz, and Sleswick-Holstein, the Elbe being their eastern boundary. It is, however, impossible to define their precise localities.

Bastarnæ (chap. 46).—The same as the Peucini.

Batavi (chap. 29).—The Batavi, originally a tribe of the Chatti, occupied what Tacitus here calls "the island of the Rhine," which (Hist. iv. 12) he explains to be the island formed by the ocean on the north, and by the Rhine on the east and west. Cæsar (Bell. Gall. iv. 10) speaks of it as the "insula Batavorum" (by which name it was generally known), and defines it rather more exactly as formed by the Rhine, the Waal, and the Meuse. It would thus be the strip of Holland on the west bank of the Rhine, from about Arnheim to Rotterdam. But the name Batavi seems to have extended beyond Cæsar's limits, and to have reached as far as Leyden ("Lugdunum Batavorum").

Boii (chap. 28)—The Boii, a Gallic tribe, occupied the eastern portion of Bavaria, and, probably, a considerable part of Bohemia, which derives its name from them.

Bructeri (chap. 33).—The original settlements of the Bructeri, from which they were driven by the Chamavi and Angrivarii, seem to have been between the Rhine and the Ems, on either side of the Lippe. Their destruction could hardly have been so complete as Tacitus represents, as they are subsequently mentioned by Claudian, "Panegyris de Quarto Consulatu Honorii," 450:—

"Venit accola silvæ
Bructerus Hercyniæ"

Buri (chap 43)—The Buri were a Suevic clan. Their settlements were in the neighbourhood of Cracow.

Chamavi (chap 33)—The Chamavi (named with the Angrivarii) seem to have been originally settled on the banks of the Ems, about Osnabruck, and probably extended westwards as far as the Weser.

Chasuarii (chap. 34)—The Chasuarii are coupled with the Dulgubini. Both tribes probably dwelt on the eastern side of the Weser, round Buckeburg.

Chatti (chap 30).—The settlements of the Chatti, one of the chief German tribes, apparently coincide with portions of Westphalia, Nassau, Hesse-Darmstadt, and Hesse-Cassel. Dr. Latham assumes the Chatti of Tacitus to be the Suevi of Cæsar. The fact that the name Chatti does not occur in Cæsar renders this hypothesis by no means improbable.

Chauci (chap. 35)—The settlements of the Chauci were, according to Tacitus, very extensive, and stretched from the North Sea, southwards, as far as the territories of the Chatti. They must, consequently, have included almost the entire country between the Ems and the Weser—that is, Oldenburg and part of Hanover—and have taken in portions of Westphalia about Munster and Paderborn.

Cherusci (chap 36).—The Cherusci were neighbours of the Chauci and Chatti. They appear to have occupied Brunswick and the south part of Hanover. Arminius, who destroyed the Roman army under Varus, was a Cheruscan chief.

Cimbri (chap. 37)—The Cimbri, in the time of Tacitus, occupied Jutland.

Dulgubini (chap. 34)—See Chasuarii.

Elisii (chap. 43).—The Elisii were a clan of the Ligii. See Ligii.

Eudoses (chap. 40).—The Eudoses were a Suevic clan. See Aviones.

Fenni (chap. 46).—The Fenni were the inhabitants of Finland.

Fosi (chap. 36).—The Fosi were neighbours of the Cherusci, probably to the north, and must have occupied part of Hanover.

Frisii (chap. 34).—The Frisii occupied the north-eastern corner of Holland.

Gothini (chap. 43).—The Gothini are probably to be placed in Silesia, about Breslau.

Gothones (chap. 43).—The Gothones probably dwelt on either side of the Vistula, the Baltic being their northern boundary. Consequently, their settlements would coincide with portions of Pomerania and Prussia Dr. Latham thinks they were identical with the Æstii

Harii (chap. 43)—The Harii were a clan of the Ligii. See Ligii.

Hellusii (chap 46)—The Hellusii (with the Oxiones) are mentioned as a fabulous tribe. Tacitus must have heard vaguely of the Finns and Laplanders.

Helvecones (chap 43).—See Ligii.

Helvetii (chap. 28).—The Helvetii, originally a Gallic tribe, crossed the Rhine, and occupied parts of what is now Baden and Wurtemburg.

Hermunduri (chap. 41)—The settlements of the Hermunduri must have been in Bavaria, and seem to have stretched from Ratisbon, northwards, as far as Bohemia and Saxony. The Saal (which Tacitus mistakes for the Elbe) has its sources in the country occupied by this tribe.

Lemovii (chap. 43).—The Lemovii dwelt on the coast, probably in the neighbourhood of Danzig. They bordered on the Gothones, to the west, as we think most probable.

Ligii (chap. 43).—The Ligii were a widely-spread tribe, comprehending several clans. Tacitus names the Harii, Helvecones, Manimi, Elisii, and Nahanarvali. Their territory was between the Oder and Vistula, and would include the greater part of Poland, and probably a portion of Silesia.

Langobardi (chap. 40).—The settlements of the Langobardi were on the west bank of the Elbe, about Luneburg.

Manimi (chap. 43).—See Ligii.

Marcomanni (chap. 43).—The Marcomanni probably occupied the southern portions of Bohemia. Marcomanni = men of the "marches."

Marsigni (chap. 43).—The Marsigni were a Suevic clan, and probably dwelt on the borders of Silesia and Bohemia, in the neighbourhood of Glatz.

Mattiaci (chap. 29).—The Mattiaci are to be placed in Nassau, about Wiesbaden So Zeuss infers from Pliny (xxxi. 2), who says that there are warm baths at Mattiacum, in Germany.

Nahanarvali (chap. 43) —See Ligii.

Naristi, Narisci (chap. 42) —The Naristi seem to have been settled about Ratisbon, between the Danube and the Bohemian frontier.

Nemetes (chap. 28).—The Nemetes are named with the Triboci and Vangiones. These tribes dwelt on the west bank of the Rhine, in what is now Rhenish Bavaria.

Nervii (chap. 28).—The Nervii dwelt on the banks of the Meuse. Cæsar speaks of them as one of the most warlike peoples of Gaul. Tacitus doubts whether they, as well as the Treveri whom he names with them, were of German origin The settlements of the Treveri were on the banks of the Moselle.

Nuithones (chap. 40).—The Nuithones were a Suevic clan. See Aviones.

Osi (chaps. 28, 43).—The Osi seem to have dwelt near the sources of the Oder and the Vistula, under the Carpathian Mountains. They would thus have occupied a part of Gallicia.

Oxiones (chap. 46).—See Hellusii.

Peucini (chap. 46).—The Peucini derived their name from the little island Peuce (Piczino), at the mouth of the Danube. Pliny (iv. 14) speaks of them as a German people bordering on the Daci. They would thus stretch through Moldavia from the Carpathian Mountains to the Black Sea Under the name Bastarnæ they are mentioned by Livy (xl. 57, 58) as a powerful people, who helped Philip, king of Macedonia, in his wars with the Romans. Plutarch ("Life of Paullus Æmilius," ch. ix.) says they were the same as the Galatæ, who dwelt round the Ister (Danube). If so, they were Gauls, which Livy also implies.

Quadi (chap. 42).—The Quadi probably occupied Moravia.

Reudigni (chap. 40).—The Reudigni were a Suevic clan See Aviones.

Rugii (chap 43).—The Rugii were a coast-tribe, and seem to have occupied the extreme north of Pomerania, about the mouth of the Oder. The Isle of Rugen is thought to have derived its name from them

Sarmatæ (chap 46)—Tacitus distinguishes the Sarmatæ from the Germans By Sarmatia he seems to have understood what is now Moldavia and Wallachia, and perhaps part of the south of Russia. He would probably have considered the Daci a branch of the Sarmatæ.

Semnones (chap 39)—The Semnones were the chief Suevic clan. Their settlements seem to have been between the Elbe and Oder, coinciding as nearly as possible with Brandenburg, and reaching possibly into Prussian Poland. Tacitus does not define their locality, but speaks of them as an important and widely-spread tribe. Velleius Paterculus (ii. 106) says that the Elbe bounded them on one side.

Sitones (chap 45)—Where the Sitones are to be placed is a matter of pure conjecture. There is nothing to indicate whether we should give the preference to Norway, Sweden, or to the eastern shores of the Baltic

Suardones (chap 40).—The Suardones were a Suevic clan. See Aviones.

Suevi (chaps 2, 38, 39).—The Suevi, according to Tacitus, occupied the larger part of Germany In fact Suevia would seem to have been a comprehensive name for the country between the Elbe and the

Vistula as far north as the Baltic. Tacitus and Cæsar differ about the Suevi (see Chatti). *Suabia* is the same word as Suevia.

Suiones (chap. 44).—The Suiones were the inhabitants of Sweden and Norway, which Tacitus supposed to be islands.

Tencteri (chap. 32)—The Tencteri are coupled with the Usipii. Both tribes were settled on the east bank of the Rhine, and seem to have occupied the neighbourhood of Coblenz, and to have extended as far as Wiesbaden, where they would touch the Mattiaci. See Mattiaci.

Treveri (chap. 28).—See Nervii.

Triboci (chap. 28).—See Nemetes.

Ubii (chap. 28).—The Ubii, originally a German people, and inhabitants of the eastern side of the Rhine (probably of Westphalia and Holland), were formed into a *colonia* by Agrippina, the wife of Claudius and mother of Nero It was known as Colonia Agrippinensis (Cologne).

Usipii (chap. 32).—See Tencteri.

Vangiones (chap. 28)—See Nemetes.

Veneti (chap. 46)—Tacitus doubts whether the Veneti were a German or Sarmatian people. Their locality is very vaguely described. Russian-Poland to the east of the Vistula probably would be included in their settlements.

GERMANY AND ITS TRIBES.

Boundaries of Germany.

Germany is separated from the Galli, the Rhæti, and Pannonii, by the rivers Rhine and Danube; mountain ranges, or the fear which each feels for the other, divide it from the Sarmatæ and Daci. Elsewhere ocean girds it, embracing broad peninsulas and islands of unexplored extent, where certain tribes and kingdoms are newly known to us, revealed by war. The Rhine springs from a precipitous and inaccessible height of the Rhætian Alps, bends slightly westward, and mingles with the Northern Ocean. The Danube pours down from the gradual and gently rising slope of Mount Abnoba, and visits many nations, to force its way at last through six channels into the Pontus; a seventh mouth is lost in marshes. CHAP. I

The inhabitants. Origin of the name "Germany."

The Germans themselves I should regard as aboriginal, and not mixed at all with other races through immigration or intercourse. For, in former times, it CHAP. II

CHAP. II was not by land but on shipboard that those who sought to emigrate would arrive; and the boundless and, so to speak, hostile ocean beyond us, is seldom entered by a sail from our world. And, beside the perils of rough and unknown seas, who would leave Asia, or Africa, or Italy for Germany, with its wild country, its inclement skies, its sullen manners and aspect, unless indeed it were his home? In their ancient songs, their only way of remembering or recording the past, they celebrate an earth-born god, Tuisco, and his son Mannus, as the origin of their race, as their founders. To Mannus they assign three sons, from whose names, they say, the coast tribes are called Ingævones; those of the interior, Herminones; all the rest, Istævones. Some, with the freedom of conjecture permitted by antiquity, assert that the god had several descendants, and the nation several appellations, as Marsi, Gambrivii, Suevi, Vandilii, and that these are genuine old names. The name Germany, on the other hand, they say, is modern and newly introduced, from the fact that the tribes which first crossed the Rhine and drove out the Gauls, and are now called Tungrians, were then called Germans. Thus what was the name of a tribe, and not of a race, gradually prevailed, till all called themselves by this self-invented name of Germans, which the conquerors had first employed to inspire terror.

The national war-songs. Legend of Ulysses.

CHAP. III. They say that Hercules, too, once visited them; and when going into battle, they sing of him first of all heroes. They have also those songs of theirs, by the recital of which ("baritus," they call it), they rouse their courage, while from the note they augur the result of the approaching conflict For, as their line shouts, they inspire or feel alarm. It is not so much an articulate sound, as a general cry of valour. They aim chiefly at a harsh note and a confused roar, putting their shields to their mouth, so that, by reverberation, it may swell into a fuller and deeper sound. Ulysses, too, is believed by some, in his long legendary wanderings, to have found his way into this ocean, and, having visited German soil, to have founded and named the town of Asciburgium, which stands on the bank of the Rhine, and is to this day inhabited. They even say that an altar dedicated to Ulysses, with the addition of the name of his father, Laertes, was formerly discovered on this same spot, and that certain monuments and tombs, with Greek inscriptions, still exist on the borders of Germany and Rhætia. These statements I have no intention of sustaining by proofs, or of refuting; every one may believe or disbelieve them as he feels inclined. CHAP III

Physical characteristics.

For my own part, I agree with those who think that the tribes of Germany are free from all taint of intermarriages with foreign nations, and that they appear as a distinct, unmixed race, like none but themselves. Hence, too, the same physical peculiarities throughout so vast a population. All have fierce blue eyes, red hair, huge frames, fit only for a sudden exertion. They are less able to bear laborious work. Heat and CHAP IV

CHAP IV. thirst they cannot in the least endure; to cold and hunger their climate and their soil inure them.

Climate and soil. Precious metals.

CHAP. V. Their country, though somewhat various in appearance, yet generally either bristles with forests or reeks with swamps; it is more rainy on the side of Gaul, bleaker on that of Noricum and Pannonia. It is productive of grain, but unfavourable to fruit-bearing trees; it is rich in flocks and herds, but these are for the most part undersized, and even the cattle have not their usual beauty or noble head. It is number that is chiefly valued; they are in fact the most highly prized, indeed the only riches of the people. Silver and gold the gods have refused to them, whether in kindness or in anger I cannot say. I would not, however, affirm that no vein of German soil produces gold or silver, for who has ever made a search? They care but little to possess or use them. You may see among them vessels of silver, which have been presented to their envoys and chieftains, held as cheap as those of clay. The border population, however, value gold and silver for their commercial utility, and are familiar with, and show preference for, some of our coins. The tribes of the interior use the simpler and more ancient practice of the barter of commodities. They like the old and well-known money, coins milled, or showing a two-horse chariot. They likewise prefer silver to gold, not from any special liking, but because a large number of silver pieces is more convenient for use among dealers in cheap and common articles.

Arms, military manœuvres, and discipline.

Even iron is not plentiful with them, as we infer from the character of their weapons. But few use swords or long lances. They carry a spear (*framea* is their name for it), with a narrow and short head, but so sharp and easy to wield that the same weapon serves, according to circumstances, for close or distant conflict. As for the horse-soldier, he is satisfied with a shield and spear; the foot-soldiers also scatter showers of missiles, each man having several and hurling them to an immense distance, and being naked or lightly clad with a little cloak. There is no display about their equipment: their shields alone are marked with very choice colours. A few only have corslets, and just one or two here and there a metal or leathern helmet. Their horses are remarkable neither for beauty nor for fleetness. Nor are they taught various evolutions after our fashion, but are driven straight forward, or so as to make one wheel to the right in such a compact body that none is left behind another. On the whole, one would say that their chief strength is in their infantry, which fights along with the cavalry; admirably adapted to the action of the latter is the swiftness of certain foot-soldiers, who are picked from the entire youth of their country, and stationed in front of the line. Their number is fixed,—a hundred from each canton; and from this they take their name among their countrymen, so that what was originally a mere number has now become a title of distinction. Their line of battle is drawn up in a wedge-like formation. To

CHAP VI give ground, provided you return to the attack, is considered prudence rather than cowardice. The bodies of their slain they carry off even in indecisive engagements. To abandon your shield is the basest of crimes, nor may a man thus disgraced be present at the sacred rites, or enter their council, many, indeed, after escaping from battle, have ended their infamy with the halter

Government. Influence of women.

CHAP VII They choose their kings by birth, their generals for merit. These kings have not unlimited or arbitrary power, and the generals do more by example than by authority. If they are energetic, if they are conspicuous, if they fight in the front, they lead because they are admired. But to reprimand, to imprison, even to flog, is permitted to the priests alone, and that not as a punishment, or at the general's bidding, but, as it were, by the mandate of the god whom they believe to inspire the warrior They also carry with them into battle certain figures and images taken from their sacred groves And what most stimulates their courage is, that their squadrons or battalions, instead of being formed by chance or by a fortuitous gathering, are composed of families and clans Close by them, too, are those dearest to them, so that they hear the shrieks of women, the cries of infants. *They* are to every man the most sacred witnesses of his bravery—*they* are his most generous applauders. The soldier brings his wounds to mother and wife, who shrink not from counting or even demanding them and who administer both food and encouragement to the combatants. CHAP. VII.

Tradition says that armies already wavering and giving way have been rallied by women who, with earnest entreaties and bosoms laid bare, have vividly represented the horrors of captivity, which the Germans fear with such extreme dread on behalf of their women, that the strongest tie by which a state can be bound is the being required to give, among the number of hostages, maidens of noble birth. They even believe that the sex has a certain sanctity and prescience, and they do not despise their counsels, or make light of their answers. In Vespasian's days we saw Veleda, long regarded by many as a divinity. In former times, too, they venerated Aurinia, and many other women, but not with servile flatteries, or with sham deification. CHAP. VIII.

Deities.

Mercury is the deity whom they chiefly worship, and on certain days they deem it right to sacrifice to him even with human victims. Hercules and Mars they appease with more lawful offerings. Some of the Suevi also sacrifice to Isis. Of the occasion and origin of this foreign rite I have discovered nothing, but that the image, which is fashioned like a light galley, indicates an imported worship. The Germans, however, do not consider it consistent with the grandeur of celestial beings to confine the gods within walls, or to liken them to the form of any human CHAP. IX.

CHAP IX. countenance. They consecrate woods and groves, and they apply the names of deities to the abstraction which they see only in spiritual worship.

Auguries and method of divination.

CHAP X Augury and divination by lot no people practise more diligently. The use of the lots is simple. A little bough is lopped off a fruit-bearing tree, and cut into small pieces; these are distinguished by certain marks, and thrown carelessly and at random over a white garment. In public questions the priest of the particular state, in private the father of the family, invokes the gods, and, with his eyes towards heaven, takes up each piece three times, and finds in them a meaning according to the mark previously impressed on them. If they prove unfavourable, there is no further consultation that day about the matter; if they sanction it, the confirmation of augury is still required. For they are also familiar with the practice of consulting the notes and the flight of birds. It is peculiar to this people to seek omens and monitions from horses. Kept at the public expense, in these same woods and groves, are white horses, pure from the taint of earthly labour; these are yoked to a sacred car, and accompanied by the priest and the king, or chief of the tribe, who note their neighings and snortings. No species of augury is more trusted, not only by the people and by the nobility, but also by the priests, who regard themselves as the ministers of the gods, and the horses as acquainted with their will. They have also another method of observing auspices, by which they seek to learn the result of an important war. Having taken, by whatever means, a prisoner from the tribe with whom they are at war, they pit him against a picked man of their own tribe, each combatant using the weapons of their country. The victory of the one or the other is accepted as an indication of the issue. CHAP. X

Councils.

About minor matters the chiefs deliberate, about the more important the whole tribe. Yet even when the final decision rests with the people, the affair is always thoroughly discussed by the chiefs. They assemble, except in the case of a sudden emergency, on certain fixed days, either at new or at full moon; for this they consider the most auspicious season for the transaction of business Instead of reckoning by days as we do, they reckon by nights, and in this manner fix both their ordinary and their legal appointments. Night they regard as bringing on day. Their freedom has this disadvantage, that they do not meet simultaneously or as they are bidden, but two or three days are wasted in the delays of assembling. When the multitude think proper, they sit down armed. Silence is proclaimed by the priests, who have on these occasions the right of keeping order. Then the king or the chief, according to age, birth, distinction in war, or eloquence, is heard, more because he has influence to persuade than because he has power to command. If his sentiments displease them, they reject them with murmurs; if they are satisfied, they brandish their spears. The most complimentary form of assent is to express approbation with their weapons. CHAP XI

Punishments. Administration of Justice.

CHAP. XII. In their councils an accusation may be preferred or a capital crime prosecuted. Penalties are distinguished according to the offence. Traitors and deserters are hanged on trees; the coward, the unwarlike, the man stained with abominable vices, is plunged into the mire of the morass, with a hurdle put over him. This distinction in punishment means that crime, they think, ought, in being punished, to be exposed, while infamy ought to be buried out of sight. Lighter offences, too, have penalties proportioned to them; he who is convicted, is fined in a certain number of horses or of cattle. Half of the fine is paid to the king or to the state, half to the person whose wrongs are avenged and to his relatives. In these same councils they also elect the chief magistrates, who administer law in the cantons and the towns. Each of these has a hundred associates chosen from the people, who support him with their advice and influence.

Training of the youth.

CHAP. XIII. They transact no public or private business without being armed. It is not, however, usual for anyone to wear arms till the state has recognised his power to use them. Then in the presence of the council one of the chiefs, or the young man's father, or some kinsman, equips him with a shield and a spear. These arms are what the "toga" is with us, the first honour with which youth is invested. Up to this time he is regarded as a member of a household, afterwards as a member of the commonwealth. Very noble birth or great services rendered by the father secure for lads the rank of a chief; such lads attach themselves to men of mature strength and of long approved valour. It is no shame to be seen among a chief's followers. Even in his escort there are gradations of rank, dependent on the choice of the man to whom they are attached. These followers vie keenly with each other as to who shall rank first with his chief, the chiefs as to who shall have the most numerous and the bravest followers. It is an honour as well as a source of strength to be thus always surrounded by a large body of picked youths; it is an ornament in peace and a defence in war. And not only in his own tribe but also in the neighbouring states it is the renown and glory of a chief to be distinguished for the number and valour of his followers, for such a man is courted by embassies, is honoured with presents, and the very prestige of his name often settles a war. CHAP XIII.

Warlike ardour of the people.

CHAP XIV. When they go into battle, it is a disgrace for the chief to be surpassed in valour, a disgrace for his followers not to equal the valour of the chief. And it is an infamy and a reproach for life to have survived the chief, and returned from the field. To defend, to protect him, to ascribe one's own brave deeds to his renown, is the height of loyalty. The chief fights for victory; his vassals fight for their chief. If their native state sinks into the sloth of prolonged peace and repose, many of its noble youths voluntarily seek those tribes which are waging some war, both because

CHAP. XIV inaction is odious to their race, and because they win renown more readily in the midst of peril, and cannot maintain a numerous following except by violence and war. Indeed, men look to the liberality of their chief for their war-horse and their blood-stained and victorious lance. Feasts and entertainments, which, though inelegant, are plentifully furnished, are their only pay. The means of this bounty come from war and rapine. Nor are they as easily persuaded to plough the earth and to wait for the year's produce as to challenge an enemy and earn the honour of wounds. Nay, they actually think it tame and stupid to acquire by the sweat of toil what they might win by their blood.

Habits in time of peace.

CHAP. XV Whenever they are not fighting, they pass much of their time in the chase, and still more in idleness, giving themselves up to sleep and to feasting, the bravest and the most warlike doing nothing, and surrendering the management of the household, of the home, and of the land, to the women, the old men, and all the weakest members of the family. They themselves lie buried in sloth, a strange combination in their nature that the same men should be so fond of idleness, so averse to peace. It is the custom of the states to bestow by voluntary and individual contribution on the chiefs a present of cattle or of grain, which, while accepted as a compliment, supplies their wants. They are particularly delighted by gifts from neighbouring tribes, which are sent not only by individuals but also by the state, such as choice steeds, heavy armour, trappings, and neck-chains. We have now taught them to accept money also. CHAP. XV.

Arrangement of their towns. Subterranean dwellings.

It is well known that the nations of Germany have no cities, and that they do not even tolerate closely contiguous dwellings. They live scattered and apart. just as a spring, a meadow, or a wood has attracted them. Their villages they do not arrange in our fashion, with the buildings connected and joined together, but every person surrounds his dwelling with an open space, either as a precaution against the disasters of fire, or because they do not know how to build. No use is made by them of stone or tile; they employ timber for all purposes, rude masses without ornament or attractiveness. Some parts of their buildings they stain more carefully with a clay so clear and bright that it resembles painting, or a coloured design. They are wont also to dig out subterranean caves, and pile on them great heaps of dung, as a shelter from winter and as a receptacle for the year's produce, for by such places they mitigate the rigour of the cold. And should an enemy approach, he lays waste the open country, while what is hidden and buried is either not known to exist, or else escapes him from the very fact that it has to be searched for. CHAP. XVI.

Dress.

They all wrap themselves in a cloak which is fastened with a clasp, or, if this is not forthcoming, with a CHAP XVII.

CHAP. XVII. thorn, leaving the rest of their persons bare. They pass whole days on the hearth by the fire. The wealthiest are distinguished by a dress which is not flowing, like that of the Sarmatæ and Parthi, but is tight, and exhibits each limb. They also wear the skins of wild beasts; the tribes on the Rhine and Danube in a careless fashion, those of the interior with more elegance, as not obtaining other clothing by commerce. These select certain animals, the hides of which they strip off and vary them with the spotted skins of beasts, the produce of the outer ocean, and of seas unknown to us. The women have the same dress as the men, except that they generally wrap themselves in linen garments, which they embroider with purple, and do not lengthen out the upper part of their clothing into sleeves. The upper and lower arm is thus bare, and the nearest part of the bosom is also exposed.

Marriage laws.

CHAP. XVIII. Their marriage code, however, is strict, and indeed no part of their manners is more praiseworthy. Almost alone among barbarians they are content with one wife, except a very few among them, and these not from sensuality, but because their noble birth procures for them many offers of alliance. The wife does not bring a dower to the husband, but the husband to the wife. The parents and relatives are present, and pass judgment on the marriage-gifts, gifts not meant to suit a woman's taste, nor such as a bride would deck herself with, but oxen, a caparisoned steed, a shield, a lance, and a sword. With these presents the wife is espoused, and she herself in her turn brings her husband a gift of arms. This they count their strongest bond of union, these their sacred mysteries, these their gods of marriage. Lest the woman should think herself to stand apart from aspirations after noble deeds and from the perils of war, she is reminded by the ceremony which inaugurates marriage that she is her husband's partner in toil and danger, destined to suffer and to dare with him alike both in peace and in war. The yoked oxen, the harnessed steed, the gift of arms, proclaim this fact She must live and die with the feeling that she is receiving what she must hand down to her children neither tarnished nor depreciated, what future daughters-in-law may receive, and may be so passed on to her grand-children. CHAP XVIII

Thus with their virtue protected they live uncorrupted by the allurements of public shows or the stimulant of feastings. Clandestine correspondence is equally unknown to men and women. Very rare for so numerous a population is adultery, the punishment for which is prompt, and in the husband's power. Having cut off the hair of the adulteress and stripped her naked, he expels her from the house in the presence of her kinsfolk, and then flogs her through the whole village. The loss of chastity meets with no indulgence; neither beauty, youth, nor wealth will procure the culprit a husband. No one in Germany laughs at vice, nor do they call it the fashion to corrupt and to be corrupted. Still better is the condition of those states in which only maidens are given in CHAP. XIX.

CHAP. XIX. marriage, and where the hopes and expectations of a bride are then finally terminated. They receive one husband, as having one body and one life, that they may have no thoughts beyond, no further-reaching desires, that they may love not so much the husband as the married state. To limit the number of their children or to destroy any of their subsequent offspring is accounted infamous, and good habits are here more effectual than good laws elsewhere.

Their children. Laws of succession

CHAP. XX. In every household the children, naked and filthy, grow up with those stout frames and limbs which we so much admire. Every mother suckles her own offspring, and never entrusts it to servants and nurses The master is not distinguished from the slave by being brought up with greater delicacy. Both live amid the same flocks and lie on the same ground till the freeborn are distinguished by age and recognised by merit. The young men marry late, and their vigour is thus unimpaired. Nor are the maidens hurried into marriage; the same age and a similar stature is required; well-matched and vigorous they wed, and the offspring reproduce the strength of the parents Sister's sons are held in as much esteem by their uncles as by their fathers; indeed, some regard the relation as even more sacred and binding, and prefer it in receiving hostages, thinking thus to secure a stronger hold on the affections and a wider bond for the family. But every man's own children are his heirs and successors, and there are no wills.

Should there be no issue, the next in succession to the property are his brothers and his uncles on either side. The more relatives he has, the more numerous his connections, the more honoured is his old age; nor are there any advantages in childlessness. CHAP XX

Hereditary feuds. Fines for homicide Hospitality.

It is a duty among them to adopt the feuds as well as the friendships of a father or a kinsman. These feuds are not implacable; even homicide is expiated by the payment of a certain number of cattle and of sheep, and the satisfaction is accepted by the entire family, greatly to the advantage of the state, since feuds are dangerous in proportion to a people's freedom. CHAP XXI.

No nation indulges more profusely in entertainments and hospitality. To exclude any human being from their roof is thought impious; every German, according to his means, receives his guest with a well-furnished table. When his supplies are exhausted, he who was but now the host becomes the guide and companion to further hospitality, and without invitation they go to the next house It matters not, they are entertained with like cordiality No one distinguishes between an acquaintance and a stranger, as regards the rights of hospitality. It is usual to give the departing guest whatever he may ask for, and a present in return is asked with as little hesitation. They are greatly charmed with gifts, but they expect no return for what they give, nor feel any obligation for what they receive.

Habits of life.

CHAP. XXII. On waking from sleep, which they generally prolong to a late hour of the day, they take a bath, oftenest of warm water, which suits a country where winter is the longest of the seasons. After their bath they take their meal, each having a separate seat and table of his own. Then they go armed to business, or no less often to their festal meetings. To pass an entire day and night in drinking disgraces no one. Their quarrels, as might be expected with intoxicated people, are seldom fought out with mere abuse, but commonly with wounds and bloodshed. Yet it is at their feasts that they generally consult on the reconciliation of enemies, on the forming of matrimonial alliances, on the choice of chiefs, finally even on peace and war, for they think that at no time is the mind more open to simplicity of purpose or more warmed to noble aspirations. A race without either natural or acquired cunning, they disclose their hidden thoughts in the freedom of the festivity. Thus the sentiments of all having been discovered and laid bare, the discussion is renewed on the following day, and from each occasion its own peculiar advantage is derived. They deliberate when they have no power to dissemble; they resolve when error is impossible.

Food.

CHAP. XXIII. A liquor for drinking is made out of barley or other grain, and fermented into a certain resemblance to wine. The dwellers on the river-bank also buy wine. Their food is of a simple kind, consisting of wild-fruit, fresh game, and curdled milk. They satisfy their hunger without elaborate preparation and without delicacies. In quenching their thirst they are not equally moderate. If you indulge their love of drinking by supplying them with as much as they desire, they will be overcome by their own vices as easily as by the arms of an enemy. CHAP. XXIII.

Sports. Passion for gambling.

One and the same kind of spectacle is always exhibited at every gathering. Naked youths who practise the sport bound in the dance amid swords and lances that threaten their lives. Experience gives them skill, and skill again gives grace; profit or pay are out of the question; however reckless their pastime, its reward is the pleasure of the spectators. Strangely enough they make games of hazard a serious occupation even when sober, and so venturesome are they about gaining or losing, that, when every other resource has failed, on the last and final throw they stake the freedom of their own persons. The loser goes into voluntary slavery; though the younger and stronger, he suffers himself to be bound and sold. Such is their stubborn persistency in a bad practice; they themselves call it honour. Slaves of this kind the owners part with in the way of commerce, and also to relieve themselves from the scandal of such a victory. CHAP. XXIV.

Slavery.

The other slaves are not employed after our manner with distinct domestic duties assigned to them, but each one has the management of a house CHAP. XXV.

CHAP. XXV. and home of his own. The master requires from the slave a certain quantity of grain, of cattle, and of clothing, as he would from a tenant, and this is the limit of subjection. All other household functions are discharged by the wife and children. To strike a slave or to punish him with bonds or with hard labour is a rare occurrence. They often kill them, not in enforcing strict discipline, but on the impulse of passion, as they would an enemy, only it is done with impunity The freedmen do not rank much above slaves, and are seldom of any weight in the family, never in the state, with the exception of those tribes which are ruled by kings There indeed they rise above the freedborn and the noble; elsewhere the inferiority of the freedman marks the freedom of the state.

Occupation of land Tillage

CHAP. XXVI. Of lending money on interest and increasing it by compound interest they know nothing,—a more effectual safeguard than if it were prohibited.

Land proportioned to the number of inhabitants is occupied by the whole community in turn, and afterwards divided among them according to rank. A wide expanse of plains makes the partition easy. They till fresh fields every year, and they have still more land than enough; with the richness and extent of their soil, they do not laboriously exert themselves in planting orchards, inclosing meadows, and watering gardens Corn is the only produce required from the earth; hence even the year itself is not divided by them into as many seasons as with us. Winter, spring, and summer have both a meaning and a name; the name and blessings of autumn are alike unknown. CHAP XXVI

Funeral rites

In their funerals there is no pomp, they simply observe the custom of burning the bodies of illustrious men with certain kinds of wood. They do not heap garments or spices on the funeral pile The arms of the dead man and in some cases his horse are consigned to the fire. A turf mound forms the tomb. Monuments with their lofty elaborate splendour they reject as oppressive to the dead. Tears and lamentations they soon dismiss; grief and sorrow but slowly It is thought becoming for women to bewail, for men to remember, the dead. CHAP XXVII.

Such on the whole is the account which I have received of the origin and manners of the entire German people. I will now touch on the institutions and religious rites of the separate tribes, pointing out how far they differ, and also what nations have migrated from Germany into Gaul

Tribes of Western Germany.

That highest authority, the great Julius, informs us that Gaul was once more powerful than Germany. Consequently we may believe that Gauls even crossed over into Germany. For what a trifling obstacle would a river be to the various tribes, as they grew in strength and wished to possess in exchange settlements which were still open to all, and not partitioned among powerful monarchies! Accordingly the country between the Hercynian forest and the rivers CHAP XXVIII.

CHAP. XXVIII

Rhine and Mœnus,[1] and that which lies beyond, was occupied respectively by the Helvetii and Boii, both tribes of Gaul. The name Boiemum still survives, marking the old tradition of the place, though the population has been changed. Whether however the Aravisci migrated into Pannonia from the Osi, a German race, or whether the Osi came from the Aravisci into Germany, as both nations still retain the same language, institutions, and customs, is a doubtful matter; for as they were once equally poor and equally free, either bank had the same attractions, the same drawbacks. The Treveri and Nervii are even eager in their claims of a German origin, thinking that the glory of this descent distinguishes them from the uniform level of Gallic effeminacy. The Rhine bank itself is occupied by tribes unquestionably German,—the Vangiones, the Triboci, and the Nemetes. Nor do even the Ubii, though they have earned the distinction of being a Roman colony, and prefer to be called Agrippinenses, from the name of their founder, blush to own their origin. Having crossed the sea in former days, and given proof of their allegiance, they were settled on the Rhine-bank itself, as those who might guard it but need not be watched.

CHAP. XXIX.

Foremost among all these nations in valour, the Batavi occupy an island within the Rhine and but a small portion of the bank. Formerly a tribe of the Chatti, they were forced by internal dissension to migrate to their present settlements and there become a part of the Roman Empire. They yet retain the

[1] The Main.

honourable badge of an ancient alliance; for they are CHAP. XXIX
not insulted by tribute, nor ground down by the tax-gatherer. Free from the usual burdens and contributions, and set apart for fighting purposes, like a magazine of arms, we reserve them for our wars The subjection of the Mattiaci is of the same character. For the greatness of the Roman people has spread reverence for our empire beyond the Rhine and the old boundaries. Thus this nation, whose settlements and territories are on their own side of the river, are yet in sentiment and purpose one with us; in all other respects they resemble the Batavi, except that they still gain from the soil and climate of their native land a keener vigour. I should not reckon among the German tribes the cultivators of the tithe-lands, although they are settled on the further side of the Rhine and Danube. Reckless adventurers from Gaul, emboldened by want, occupied this land of questionable ownership After a while, our frontier having been advanced, and our military positions pushed forward, it was regarded as a remote nook of our empire and a part of a Roman province.

Beyond them are the Chatti, whose settlements begin CHAP. XXX.
at the Hercynian forest, where the country is not so open and marshy as in the other cantons into which Germany stretches. They are found where there are hills, and with them grow less frequent, for the Hercynian forest keeps close till it has seen the last of its native Chatti. Hardy frames, close-knit limbs, fierce countenances, and a peculiarly vigorous courage, mark the tribe. For Germans, they have much

CHAP XXX intelligence and sagacity; they promote their picked men to power, and obey those whom they promote; they keep their ranks, note their opportunities, check their impulses, portion out the day, intrench themselves by night, regard fortune as a doubtful, valour as an unfailing, resource; and what is most unusual, and only given to systematic discipline, they rely more on the general than on the army. Their whole strength is in their infantry, which, in addition to its arms, is laden with iron tools and provisions. Other tribes you see going to battle, the Chatti to a campaign. Seldom do they engage in mere raids and casual encounters. It is indeed the peculiarity of a cavalry force quickly to win and as quickly to yield a victory. Fleetness and timidity go together; deliberateness is more akin to steady courage.

CHAP XXXI. A practice, rare among the other German tribes, and simply characteristic of individual prowess, has become general among the Chatti, of letting the hair and beard grow as soon as they have attained manhood, and not till they have slain a foe laying aside that peculiar aspect which devotes and pledges them to valour. Over the spoiled and bleeding enemy they show their faces once more; then, and not till then, proclaiming that they have discharged the obligations of their birth, and proved themselves worthy of their country and of their parents. The coward and the unwarlike remain unshorn. The bravest of them also wear an iron ring (which otherwise is a mark of disgrace among the people) until they have released themselves by the slaughter of a foe. Most of the Chatti delight in these fashions. Even hoary-headed men are distinguished by them, and are thus conspicuous alike to enemies and to fellow-countrymen. To begin the battle always rests with *them*; *they* form the first line, an unusual spectacle. Nor even in peace do they assume a more civilised aspect. They have no home or land or occupation; they are supported by whomsoever they visit, as lavish of the property of others as they are regardless of their own, till at length the feebleness of age makes them unequal to so stern a valour. CHAP. XXXI.

Next to the Chatti on the Rhine, which has now a well-defined channel, and serves as a boundary, dwell the Usipii and Tencteri. The latter, besides the more usual military distinctions, particularly excel in the organisation of cavalry, and the Chatti are not more famous for their foot-soldiers than are the Tencteri for their horsemen. What their forefathers originated, posterity maintain. This supplies sport to their children, rivalry to their youths: even the aged keep it up. Horses are bequeathed along with the slaves, the dwelling-house, and the usual rights of inheritance; they go to the son, not to the eldest, as does the other property, but to the most warlike and courageous. CHAP. XXXII.

After the Tencteri came, in former days, the Bructeri; but the general account now is, that the Chamavi and Angrivarii entered their settlements, drove them out and utterly exterminated them with the common help of the neighbouring tribes, either from hatred of their CHAP. XXXIII.

CHAP. XXXIII. tyranny, or from the attractions of plunder, or from heaven's favourable regard for us. It did not even grudge us the spectacle of the conflict. More than sixty thousand fell, not beneath the Roman arms and weapons, but, grander far, before our delighted eyes. May the tribes, I pray, ever retain if not love for us, at least hatred for each other; for while the destinies of empire hurry us on, fortune can give no greater boon than discord among our foes.

CHAP. XXXIV. The Angrivarii and Chamavi are bounded in the rear by the Dulgubini and Chasuarii, and other tribes not equally famous. Towards the river are the Frisii, distinguished as the Greater and Lesser Frisii, according to their strength. Both these tribes, as far as the ocean, are skirted by the Rhine, and their territory also embraces vast lakes which Roman fleets have navigated. We have even ventured on the ocean itself in these parts Pillars of Hercules, so rumour commonly says. still exist; whether Hercules really visited the country, or whether we have agreed to ascribe every work of grandeur, wherever met with, to his renown. Drusus Germanicus indeed did not lack daring; but the ocean barred the explorer's access to itself and to Hercules. Subsequently no one has made the attempt, and it has been thought more pious and reverential to believe in the actions of the gods than to inquire

Northern tribes.

CHAP. XXXV. Thus far we have taken note of Western Germany. Northwards the country takes a vast sweep. First

comes the tribe of the Chauci, which, beginning at the CHAP XXXV
Frisian settlements, and occupying a part of the coast, stretches along the frontier of all the tribes which I have enumerated, till it reaches with a bend as far as the Chatti. This vast extent of country is not merely possessed, but densely peopled, by the Chauci, the noblest of the German races, a nation who would maintain their greatness by righteous dealing. Without ambition, without lawless violence, they live peaceful and secluded, never provoking a war or injuring others by rapine and robbery. Indeed, the crowning proof of their valour and their strength is, that they keep up their superiority without harm to others. Yet all have their weapons in readiness, and an army if necessary, with a multitude of men and horses; and even while at peace they have the same renown of valour.

Dwelling on one side of the Chauci and Chatti, the CHAP XXXVI
Cherusci long cherished, unassailed, an excessive and enervating love of peace. This was more pleasant than safe, for to be peaceful is self-deception among lawless and powerful neighbours. Where the strong hand decides, moderation and justice are terms applied only to the more powerful; and so the Cherusci, ever reputed good and just, are now called cowards and fools, while in the case of the victorious Chatti success has been identified with prudence. The downfall of the Cherusci brought with it also that of the Fosi, a neighbouring tribe, which shared equally in their disasters, though they had been inferior to them in prosperous days.

In the same remote corner of Germany, bordering on the ocean dwell the Cimbri, a now insignificant tribe, but of great renown. Of their ancient glory wide-spread traces yet remain; on both sides of the Rhine are encampments of vast extent, and by their circuit you may even now measure the war-like strength of the tribe, and find evidence of that mighty emigration. Rome was in her 640th year when we first heard of the Cimbrian invader in the consulship of Cæcilius Metellus and Papirius Carbo, from which time to the second consulship of the Emperor Trajan we have to reckon about 210 years. So long have we been in conquering Germany. In the space of this long epoch many losses have been sustained on both sides. Neither Samnite nor Carthaginian, neither Spain nor Gaul, not even the Parthians, have given us more frequent warnings. German independence truly is fiercer than the des-potism of an Arsaces. What else, indeed, can the East taunt us with but the slaughter of Crassus, when it has itself lost Pacorus, and been crushed under a Ventidius? But Germans, by routing or making prisoners of Carbo, Cassius, Scaurus Aurelius, Servilius Cæpio, and Marcus Manlius, deprived the Roman people of five consular armies, and they robbed even a Cæsar of Varus and his three legions. Not without loss to us were they discomfited by Marius in Italy, by the great Julius in Gaul, and by Drusus, Nero, and Germanicus, on their own ground Soon after, the mighty menaces of Caius Cæsar were turned into a jest. Then came a lull, until on the occasion of our discords and the civil war, they stormed the winter camp of our legions, and even designed the conquest of Gaul. Again were they driven back; and in recent times we have celebrated triumphs rather than won conquests over them. CHAP XXXVII.

The Suevi and kindred tribes.

I must now speak of the Suevi, who are not one nation as are the Chatti and Tencteri, for they occupy the greater part of Germany, and have hitherto been divided into separate tribes with names of their own, though they are called by the general designation of "Suevi." A national peculiarity with them is to twist their hair back, and fasten it in a knot. This distinguishes the Suevi from the other Germans, as it also does their own freeborn from their slaves. With other tribes, either from some connection with the Suevic race, or, as often happens, from imitation, the practice is an occasional one, and restricted to youth. The Suevi, till their heads are grey, affect the fashion of drawing back their unkempt locks, and often they are knotted on the very top of the head. The chiefs have a more elaborate style; so much do they study appearance, but in perfect innocence, not with any thoughts of love-making; but arranging their hair when they go to battle, to make themselves tall and terrible, they adorn themselves, so to speak, for the eyes of the foe. CHAP XXXVIII

The Semnones give themselves out to be the most ancient and renowned branch of the Suevi. Their antiquity is strongly attested by their religion. At a stated period, all the tribes of the same race assemble CHAP XXXIX

CHAP. XXXIX. by their representatives in a grove consecrated by the auguries of their forefathers, and by immemorial associations of terror. Here, having publicly slaughtered a human victim, they celebrate the horrible beginning of their barbarous rite Reverence also in other ways is paid to the grove. No one enters it except bound with a chain, as an inferior acknowledging the might of the local divinity. If he chance to fall, it is not lawful for him to be lifted up, or to rise to his feet, he must crawl out along the ground. All this superstition implies the belief that from this spot the nation took its origin, that here dwells the supreme and all-ruling deity, to whom all else is subject and obedient The fortunate lot of the Semnones strengthens this belief; a hundred cantons are in their occupation, and the vastness of their community makes them regard themselves as the head of the Suevic race.

CHAP. XL. To the Langobardi, on the contrary, their scanty numbers are a distinction. Though surrounded by a host of most powerful tribes, they are safe, not by submitting, but by daring the perils of war. Next come the Reudigni, the Aviones, the Anglii, the Varini, the Eudoses, the Suardones, and Nuithones who are fenced in by rivers or forests. None of these tribes have any noteworthy feature, except their common worship of Ertha, or mother-Earth, and their belief that she interposes in human affairs, and visits the nations in her car. In an island of the ocean there is a sacred grove, and within it a consecrated chariot, covered over with a garment. Only one priest is permitted to touch it. *He* can perceive the presence of the goddess in this sacred recess, and walks by her side with the utmost reverence as she is drawn along by heifers. It is a season of rejoicing, and festivity reigns wherever she deigns to go and be received. They do not go to battle or wear arms, every weapon is under lock; peace and quiet are known and welcomed only at these times, till the goddess, weary of human intercourse, is at length restored by the same priest to her temple. Afterwards the car, the vestments, and, if you like to believe it, the divinity herself, are purified in a secret lake Slaves perform the rite, who are instantly swallowed up by its waters. Hence arises a mysterious terror and a pious ignorance concerning the nature of that which is seen only by men doomed to die. This branch indeed of the Suevi stretches into the remoter regions of Germany. CHAP XL.

Tribes along the Danube and in the East of Germany

Nearer to us is the state of the Hermunduri (I shall follow the course of the Danube as I did before that of the Rhine), a people loyal to Rome. Consequently they, alone of the Germans, trade not merely on the banks of the river, but far inland, and in the most flourishing colony of the province of Rætia. Everywhere they are allowed to pass without a guard; and while to the other tribes we display only our arms and our camps, to them we have thrown open our houses and country-seats, which they do not covet. It is in their lands that the Elbe takes its rise, a famous river known to us in past days; now we only hear of it. CHAP XLI.

CHAP XLII. The Narisci border on the Hermunduri, and then follow the Marcomanni and Quadi. The Marcomanni stand first in strength and renown, and their very territory, from which the Boii were driven in a former age, was won by valour. Nor are the Narisci and Quadi inferior to them. This I may call the frontier of Germany, so far as it is completed by the Danube. The Marcomanni and Quadi have, up to our time, been ruled by kings of their own nation, descended from the noble stock of Maroboduus and Tudrus. They now submit even to foreigners, but the strength and power of the monarch depend on Roman influence. He is occasionally supported by our arms, more frequently by our money, and his authority is none the less

CHAP. XLIII. Behind them the Marsigni, Gotini, Osi, and Buri, close in the rear of the Marcomanni and Quadi. Of these, the Marsigni and Buri, in their language and manner of life, resemble the Suevi. The Gotini and Osi are proved by their respective Gallic and Pannonian tongues, as well as by the fact of their enduring tribute, not to be Germans. Tribute is imposed on them as aliens, partly by the Sarmatæ, partly by the Quadi. The Gotini, to complete their degradation, actually work iron mines. All these nations occupy but little of the plain country, dwelling in forests and on mountain-tops. For Suevia is divided and cut in half by a continuous mountain-range, beyond which live a multitude of tribes. The name of Ligii, spread as it is among many states, is the most widely extended. It will be enough to mention the most powerful, which are the Harii, the Helvecones, the Manimi, the Helisii and the Nahanarvali. Among these last is shown a grove of immemorial sanctity. A priest in female attire has the charge of it. But the deities are described in Roman language as Castor and Pollux. Such, indeed, are the attributes of the divinity, the name being Alcis. They have no images, or, indeed, any vestige of foreign superstition, but it is as brothers and as youths that the deities are worshipped. The Harii, besides being superior in strength to the tribes just enumerated, savage as they are, make the most of their natural ferocity by the help of art and opportunity. Their shields are black, their bodies dyed. They choose dark nights for battle, and, by the dread and gloomy aspect of their death-like host, strike terror into the foe, who can never confront their strange and almost infernal appearance. For in all battles it is the eye which is first vanquished. CHAP. XLIII.

Remaining tribes.

Beyond the Ligii are the Gothones, who are ruled by kings, a little more strictly than the other German tribes, but not as yet inconsistently with freedom. Immediately adjoining them, further from the coast, are the Rugii and Lemovii, the badge of all these tribes being the round shield, the short sword, and servile submission to their kings. CHAP. XLIV.

And now begin the states of the Suiones, situated on the Ocean itself, and these, besides men and arms, are powerful in ships. The form of their vessels is peculiar in this respect, that a prow at either extremity acts as a forepart, always ready for running into shore.

CHAP. XLIV. They are not worked by sails, nor have they a row of oars attached to their sides; but, as on some rivers, the apparatus of rowing is unfixed, and shifted from side to side as circumstances require. And they likewise honour wealth, and so a single ruler holds sway with no restrictions, and with no uncertain claim to obedience. Arms are not with them, as with the other Germans, at the general disposal, but are in the charge of a keeper, who is actually a slave; for the ocean forbids the sudden inroad of enemies, and, besides, an idle multitude of armed men is easily demoralized. And indeed it is by no means the policy of a monarch to place either a nobleman, a freeborn citizen, or even a freedman, at the head of an armed force.

CHAP. XLV. Beyond the Suiones is another sea, sluggish and almost motionless, which, we may certainly infer, girdles and surrounds the world, from the fact that the last radiance of the setting sun lingers on till sunrise, with a brightness sufficient to dim the light of the stars. Even the very sound of his rising, as popular belief adds, may be heard, and the forms of gods and the glory round his head may be seen. Only thus far (and here rumour seems truth) does the world extend.

At this point the Suevic sea, on its eastern shore, washes the tribes of the Æstii, whose rites and fashions and style of dress are those of the Suevi, while their language is more like the British. They worship the mother of the gods, and wear as a religious symbol the device of a wild boar. This serves as armour, and as a universal defence, rendering the votary of the goddess safe even amidst enemies. They often use clubs, iron weapons but seldom. They are more patient in cultivating corn and other produce than might be expected from the general indolence of the Germans. But they also search the deep, and are the only people who gather amber (which they call "glesum"), in the shallows, and also on the shore itself. Barbarians as they are they have not investigated or discovered what natural cause or process produces it. Nay, it even lay amid the sea's other refuse, till our luxury gave it a name. To them it is utterly useless; they gather it in its raw state, bring it to us in shapeless lumps, and marvel at the price which they receive. It is however a juice from trees, as you may infer from the fact that there are often seen shining through it, reptiles, and even winged insects, which, having become entangled in the fluid, are gradually enclosed in the substance as it hardens. I am therefore inclined to think that the islands and countries of the West, like the remote recesses of the East, where frankincense and balsam exude, contain fruitful woods and groves; that these productions, acted on by the near rays of the sun, glide in a liquid state into the adjacent sea, and are thrown up by the force of storms on the opposite shores. If you test the composition of amber by applying fire, it burns like pinewood, and sends forth a rich and fragrant flame; it is soon softened into something like pitch or resin.

Closely bordering on the Suiones are the tribes of the Sitones, which, resembling them in all else, differ only in being ruled by a woman. So low

CHAP. XLV. have they fallen, not merely from freedom, but even from slavery itself. Here Suevia ends.

CHAP XLVI As to the tribes of the Peucini, Veneti, and Fenni, I am in doubt whether I should class them with the Germans or the Sarmatæ, although indeed the Peucini called by some Bastarnæ, are like Germans in their language, mode of life, and in the permanence of their settlements. They all live in filth and sloth, and by the intermarriages of the chiefs they are becoming in some degree debased into a resemblance to the Sarmatæ. The Veneti have borrowed largely from the Sarmatian character; in their plundering expeditions they roam over the whole extent of forest and mountain between the Peucini and Fenni. They are however to be rather referred to the German race, for they have fixed habitations, carry shields, and delight in strength and fleetness of foot, thus presenting a complete contrast to the Sarmatæ, who live in waggons and on horseback. The Fenni are strangely beastlike and squalidly poor; neither arms nor homes have they; their food is herbs, their clothing skins, their bed the earth. They trust wholly to their arrows, which, for want of iron, are pointed with bone. The men and the women are alike supplied by the chase; for the latter are always present, and demand a share of the prey. The little children have no shelter from wild beasts and storms but a covering of interlaced boughs Such are the homes of the young, such the resting place of the old. Yet they count this greater happiness than groaning over field-labour, toiling at building, and poising the fortunes of themselves and others between hope and fear. Heedless of men, heedless of gods, they have attained that hardest of results, the not needing so much as a wish. All else is fabulous, as that the Hellusii and Oxiones have the faces and expressions of men, with the bodies and limbs of wild beasts. All this is unauthenticated, and I shall leave it open. CHAP XLVI

NOTES TO THE GERMANY.

Thus what was the name of a tribe and not of a race gradually prevailed till all called themselves by the self-invented name of Germans, which the conquerors had first employed to inspire terror. (Ita nationis nomen non gentis evaluisse paullatim, ut omnes, primum a victore ob metum mox etiam a se ipsis invento nomine Germani vocarentur.)

CHAP. II. This is an obscure sentence There is great difficulty about the words "a victore ob metum," which have been variously explained It seems hardly possible that the preposition *a* can have the two distinct meanings of "from" and "by" in the same sentence; and whatever be its meaning in "a se ipsis," must, one would think, be its meaning in "a victore." If "a se ipsis" means, as it would appear to do, "they were called Germans by themselves when the name had once been found for them," "a victore" must mean they were so called by the conqueror. But then comes the difficulty about the words "ob metum," which, to suit the sense, have generally been explained as if they were equivalent to "ut metum ceteris tacerent," or to "metûs injiciendi causâ." This is a very strange meaning for the words to bear, and we cannot think of any precisely similar expression. Orelli says it is better to take them intransitively, and he compares two passages in the Annals, i. 1 and i. 68: "Res ob metum falsæ," "milite quasi ob metum defixo" In these passages the meaning of "ob metum" is perfectly clear, but we cannot see that it throws much light on the present passage. All we can make of the words is that they mean, "on account of the fear felt all round for the conquering tribe, and for the other tribes which had not yet crossed the Rhine." That is to say, "They were all at first called Germans by the conquering tribe, because of the fear inspired by the name." The conquerors took advantage of the panic which they had spread among the conquered, and said they were only a part of a great German people beyond the Rhine CHAP II

Tacitus is here in agreement with Cæsar, who says (Bell. Gall ii. 4) that the first of the emigrants from Germany were the Condrusi, Eburones, Cæræsi, and Pæmani, who were called by the common name of Germans. A large part of the Belgæ were of German origin.

German is said to be Wehr-mann—a warrior or man of war, and this etymology of the word has been used to explain "ob metum"

Or even demanding them (exigere plagas).

This phrase has been variously rendered. It has been interpreted to mean examining the wounds and comparing them together, with the view of ascertain- CHAP VII

CHAP. VII. ing who returned from battle with the most honourable scars. This version is approved by Orelli. In Bohn's edition of the Oxford translation the words are rendered "to search out the gashes," in which sense Ritter takes them, who says they mean, "examining the wounds to see whether they are dangerous." We doubt if "exigere" will bear this meaning. We prefer Gronovius's interpretation, "demanding wounds as a test of valour." It seems to suit the context best, and to give the force of the word "exigere."

Veleda.

CHAP. VIII. Veleda is mentioned, Hist. iv. 61. She is said to have been a maiden of the Bructeri, to have possessed extensive dominion, and to have raised her power to a great height by having foretold the success of the Germans and destruction of the Roman legions. This was in the reign of Vespasian, and her prophecy was fulfilled by Civilis.

The sham of deification (tamquam facerent deas).

According to Hist. iv. 61, the Germans attributed to some of their women actual divinity. So that here Tacitus must mean that they worshipped certain women, really believing them to be divine, not to flatter them in the spirit of an idle adulation, which at Rome had prompted the Senate to deify Caius Cæsar's sister, Drusilla, and Poppæa, Sabina's daughter by Nero, who lived but four months. There can be little doubt but that Tacitus had in his mind these shameful instances of servility.

The cantons and towns (pagos vicosque).

The word "pagus" denotes a district, a canton. The territory of each tribe was divided into so many "pagi." These again would include a number of "vici," towns or villages. Compare Ann. i. 56, where the two words are connected. CHAP. XII.

To earn the honour of wounds (vulnera mereri).

This expression rather confirms us in the view which we have taken of "exigere plagas." It clearly implies that wounds received in battle were looked upon as an honourable distinction. CHAP. XIV.

Much of their time in the chase, and still more in idleness (multum venatibus, plus per otium).

We think with Kritz that "non multum" (which Orelli reads) is intolerably awkward, to say nothing of its being in direct contradiction to Cæsar, who (Bell. Gall. vi. 21) speaks of the Germans as devoting themselves *wholly* to the chase and to warfare, and (iv. 1) says that the Suevi spent much of their time in hunting ("multum sunt in venationibus"). One would expect a roving and warlike people to be partial to the chase. CHAP. XV.

Nor do they call it the fashion to corrupt and be corrupted (nec corrumpere et corrumpi sæculum vocatur).

"Sæculum" is here almost equivalent to "mores." It means "the way of the world," or "the conventional standard of morals. Louandre renders it "la mode du siècle." We may compare the New Testament sense of *αἰών*. CHAP. XIX.

CHAP. XIX. *To limit the number of their children, &c.* (*Numerum liberorum finire aut quemquam ex agnatis necare*).

See note, Agric. 6.

Good habits are here more effectual than good laws elsewhere.

This is probably an allusion to the "Lex Julia," the object of which was to encourage marriage.

Nor are there any advantages in childlessness (*nec ulla orbitatis pretia*).

CHAP. XX. Tacitus implies that in the corrupt society of Rome the advantages of childlessness were very great. The rich and childless were notoriously a mark for polite attentions, as Horace and Juvenal tell us. Pliny says (Epist iv. 15) that in his time such were the prizes within reach of the childless ("orbitatis præmia") that it was thought a burden and a disadvantage to have even a single son.

Increasing it by compound interest (*in usuras extendere*).

CHAP. XXVI. We think (with Orelli and Ritter) this must be the meaning of the words, though they have been taken differently. It seems perfectly certain that they cannot be a mere repetition of "fenus agitare," as they are made to be in the Oxford translation. Nor do we like Walther's explanation of them, which is, lending money out during a long period of time and exacting the interest at regular stated intervals. Is not this fairly implied in the words "fenus agitare" by themselves?

Land proportioned to the number of inhabitants is occupied by the whole community in turn, and afterwards divided among them according to rank. (*Agri, pro numero cultorum, ab universis in vices occupantur, quos mox inter se, secundum dignationem partiuntur*)

This is a passage of well-known difficulty. Ritter, partly on the strength of what Tacitus tells us (ch. 16) about the Germans living in wide straggling villages, reads "in vicos" for "in vices." But "in vicos occupantur" is such a harsh expression, that we think it ought not to be admitted without some very good reason. Ritter takes it as an equivalent to "ut fiant vici" ("the lands are occupied so as to form villages"), and quotes as similar phrases "*in* hos artus, *in* hæc corpora excrescunt" (ch. 20); "partem vestibus *in* manicas extendunt" (17); "nec remos *in* ordinem lateribus adjungunt" (44); "ut *in* picem lentescit" (45). Not one of these instances seems to us a fair parallel, and we prefer Orelli's "in vices," though difficult of explanation. We believe Tacitus is speaking, not of the legal tenure of land generally among the Germans, but simply of the manner in which it was occupied for the purposes of tillage. He has certainly told us (ch. 16) that "they live scattered and apart, as a spring, a meadow, or a wood has attracted them;" and though Cæsar says expressly (Bell. Gall. iv. 1) that they have no private or separate landed possessions, something of the kind seems to be recognised in the words just quoted. At any rate it is difficult to see how they can be reconciled with the idea of a perpetual change of occupancy. CHAP XXVI

K

CHAP. XXVI. which seems implied in the present passage. Whether Tacitus (in ch. 16) means to assert in contradiction to Cæsar that there were fixed properties in Germany or not, *here* he must be speaking of land held by the whole community (what the Romans called "ager publicus"); which land, he says, was portioned out (possibly by lot) for cultivation among the people according to their number, the distribution of the allotments being changed from time to time. The land was first simply portioned out; the next step ("mox") was to assign larger portions to the chiefs and nobles. The whole, however, as we understand it, continued to be "ager publicus." An arrangement, otherwise impossible, was rendered easy by the vast extent of the country. The passage, thus understood, agrees substantially with what Cæsar says (Bell. Gall. vi. 22) that none of the Germans has his own proper and fixed amount of land, but that the magistrates assign every year to families and clans settled on the same spot, as much as they think fit, and wherever they choose, and compel them in the course of a year to go elsewhere.

They till fresh fields every year. (*Arva per annos mutant*)

As nothing but corn was grown, they did not get a second crop on the same land without letting it lie fallow for a year. Consequently they grew their corn on fresh land every year, which they could, under the circumstances explained, easily do. "Arva" means arable land, as distinguished from wood and pasture.

Except that they still gain from the soil and climate of their native land a keener vigour (nisi quod ipso adhuc terræ suæ solo et cælo acrius animantur).

The expression "acrius animantur" seems to include the ideas of "enterprise" and courage. "Adhuc" must mean "up to the present time," and so far as Tacitus could speak of them. CHAP. XXIX.

The Mattiaci lived on high ground, and in a clear, sharp air, compared with the Batavi. The air of the "insula Batavorum" was thick and cloudy.

The tithe-lands. (Decumates agri.)

The word "decumates" is found nowhere else; but we have the similar forms "infernates" and "supernates" in Pliny. It must mean the same as "decumanus," although Ritter tries to distinguish them by restricting "decumanus ager" to land in a corn-producing province, while these "decumates agri" were no part of a province, but simply an addition to Upper Germany. But there seems no good reason for thinking that Tacitus used this particular form to imply such a distinction. All he means is land for the occupation of which (under Roman protection) the cultivators paid a tenth of the produce. By the expression "questionable ownership," is meant that it was a debateable land between the Gauls and Germans. In the time of Tacitus it was a march or military frontier, and the tithes probably went to the maintenance of Roman armies and garrisons in the adjacent provinces. It is not clear whether by the words "pars provinciæ" Tacitus means part of

CHAP. XXIX. Rætia (which was immediately to the south), or part of Upper Germany which was to the west. One would suppose that these lands might be looked on as situated in both provinces. Speaking roughly, the "decumates agri" would coincide with part of the Duchy of Baden, part of Wurtemburg, and a small portion of Bavaria.

It was in the reign of Trajan that the Roman frontier was advanced in these parts. That emperor began a fortified line, which was afterwards completed, from the Rhine to the Danube. This great work was carried from Ratisbon to Mayence. It was known as Trajan's wall. It may still be traced to some extent by the marks of a mound and a ditch. This explains the words "limite acto."

They are found where there are hills, and with them grow less frequent, for the Hercynian forest keeps close till it has seen the last of its native Chatti. (Durant siquidem colles, paullatimque rarescunt; et Cattos suos saltus Hercynius prosequitur simul atque deponit.)

CHAP. XXX. This we have no doubt is Tacitus's meaning, though his language is harsh and embarrassing. We take the sentence as if it stood thus: "Durant, siquidem colles durant, paullatim rarescunt siquidem colles rarescunt.

We think "Chatti" is the nominative to "durant," which word we believe to be simply equivalent to "vivunt," in which use it occasionally occurs in Tacitus. It hardly seems necessary to explain it as Orelli does: "they continue to dwell from necessity." The word, we think, may be fairly applied both to the people and to the range of hills. The meaning of "deponit" is clear enough, but it is an extremely bold and rhetorical expression. CHAP XXX

Check their impulses (differre impetus).

"Differre" means to "put off, defer;" hence it comes to the same thing as "to restrain, to check" It is thus rendered in the Oxford translation, "restrain impetuous motions."

A practice rare among the other German tribes, and simply characteristic of individual prowess, has become general among the Chatti, of letting their hair and beard grow as soon as they have attained manhood, and not till they have slain a foe laying aside that peculiar aspect which devotes and pledges them to valour.

There is an apt illustration of this passage in Hist. iv. 61: "Then Civilis fulfilled a vow often made by barbarians: his hair, which he had let grow long and coloured with a red dye, from the day of taking up arms against Rome, he now cut short, when the destruction of the legions had been accomplished." CHAP. XXXI

Even hoary-headed men are distinguished by them, and are thus conspicuous alike to enemies and fellow-countrymen. (Jamque canent insignes, et hostibus simul suisque monstrati).

It is difficult in a translation to preserve the full force of the original, which has a bold and almost

CHAP. XXXI. poetic turn. "Insignes" is equivalent to a participle, and stands for "hoc modo insigniti." "Monstrati" (marked out) is used as in Agric. 13, "monstratus fatis Vespasianus."

While the destinies of empire hurry us on (*urgentibus imperii fatis*).

CHAP. XXXIII. It is doubtful whether "urgere" means to hurry on the extension of the empire or "to weigh down and press hard." Orelli prefers the first view, and, assuming that Tacitus wrote the Germania in the reign of Trajan, it is probably correct. The empire was then, to all appearance, powerful and prosperous; but Tacitus may have thought he saw danger in the policy of aggrandizement to which it was committed. Ritter takes "urgere" in the sense of "to weigh down," and he thinks the allusion is to the disasters of the war with Civilis, and to the horrors of Domitian's reign. Possibly there is an intentional vagueness about the word "urgentibus," and the two ideas of an inevitable extension of the frontiers and of being driven on to unknown dangers may be combined in it. Lipsius preferred the reading "vergentibus," which was adopted by Gronovius, in the sense, "the destinies of our empire being on the wane." It has, however, hardly any authority. Nor can we see any good reason for the reading which Kritz has adopted, "*in* urgentibus imperii fatis," and which he explains to mean, "should dangerous times hereafter threaten the empire." It does not seem so simple, or to yield as apt a sense, as the reading we have followed.

Northwards the country takes a vast sweep (*in septentrionem ingenti flexu redit*).

In ch. 1 he has spoken of broad promontories ("latos sinus"), and in 37, "the remote corner where the Cimbri dwell bordering on the ocean," is the same as what he here describes by the words "ingenti flexu." He means Jutland and the duchies of Sleswick-Holstein. The peculiar force of the word "redit" is, that the land, after running up northwards, returns, so to speak, or bends back. It is used in a similar manner by Virgil, Georg iii. 351:— CHAP. XXXV.

"Quaque redit medium Rhodope porrecta sub axem."

Even designed the conquest of Gaul (*etiam Gallias affectavere.*

The reference is to the civil wars, first between Otho and Vitellius, and then between Vitellius and Vespasian, of which last Civilis took advantage, thinking to rouse Gaul as well as Germany against the Romans. In Hist. iv. 18 we are told that he was bent on the ultimate conquest of Gaul and Germany. CHAP. XXXVII

In recent times we have celebrated triumphs rather than won conquests over them

Tacitus here alludes sneeringly to Domitian's triumph over the Chatti, which in the Agricola 39 he characterises as a contemptible affair, at which everybody laughed.

The Suevi till their heads are grey affect the fashion of drawing back their unkempt locks (apud Suevos ad canitiem horrentem capillum retro sequuntur).

CHAP. XXXVIII. We think the word "sequuntur" must be used here as it is in ch. 5: "argentum magis quam aurum sequuntur." The interpretation of Orelli (who takes "retro" with "sequuntur"), "they let their hair grow long, and twist it back from their neck and shoulders to the top of their head," can hardly be got out of the words. We suppose "retro" must be joined with "horrentem," though the word hardly seems in its right place. There can, we think, be no doubt that "horrentem" should be construed with "capillum," and not with "canitiem," as some take it.

The Elbe (Albis).

CHAP. XLI. Tacitus seems to be confounding the Saale with the Elbe, of which it is a tributary. The Elbe was the furthest limit, eastwards and northwards, to which the Roman arms advanced in Germany. Claudius Drusus (B.C. 9) reached it, but did not cross it. Domitius Ahenobarbus, Nero's grandfather, as we learn from Ann. iv. 44, crossed the river, and thus penetrated further into Germany than any other Roman had hitherto done. This was B.C. 3, and it was followed by an expedition two years later, under the same command, to the banks of the Lower Albis. Never afterwards did a Roman army advance so far in this direction.

The Gotini, to complete their degradation, actually work iron mines.

Aikin has a good note on this passage—"I should imagine that the expression 'quo magis pudeat' does not refer merely to the slavery of working in mines, but to the circumstance of their digging up iron, the substance by means of which they might acquire freedom and independence. This is quite in the manner of Tacitus. The word 'iron' was figuratively used by the ancients to signify military force in general. Thus Solon, in his well-known answer to Crœsus, observed to him that 'the nation which possessed more iron would be master of all the gold.'" CHAP XLIII

And so a single ruler holds sway with no restrictions (eoque unus imperitat nullis jam exceptionibus).

There were such restrictions among the other German tribes (see ch. 7); there were none among the Suevi. The force of the word "jam" is that as you go northwards, the people degenerate more and more from the spirit of liberty which characterises the southern tribes. We see no ground in these words for the inference drawn from them by Spener (Notit. Germ. Antiq) that the crown among the Suevi was hereditary, and not elective. CHAP XLIV

Tacitus no doubt mentions the honour which the Suevi pay to wealth because they were, in this respect, a contrast to all the other tribes.

A DIALOGUE ON ORATORY.

INTRODUCTION

TO THE DIALOGUE ON ORATORY.

THIS Dialogue is intended as a discussion of the question whether the oratory of the imperial, and particularly the Flavian, age was inferior to that of the last days of the republic, and, if so, why so? It is, we believe, seldom read. Unfortunately the text is rather corrupt, and there are some serious *lacunae*. Its genuineness, too, has always been a matter of doubt and controversy. It is true, indeed, that the old MSS assign it to Tacitus, and there really do not seem to be any very solid or definite grounds for deciding against his authorship. Most scholars, Orelli and Ritter among the number, incline to this view. Ingenious critics have attributed it to Quintilian, or to the younger Pliny, but, as far as we can see, without the semblance of anything that can be called evidence. It can hardly be argued that the style is at all pointedly unlike that of the Annals and History, and it may fairly be said that here and there may be traced resemblances. It is noted by Orelli that one of the letters of the younger Pliny, addressed to Tacitus, suggests the idea that Pliny was reminding his friend of an expression he had used in this very Dialogue. "Poetry," he says, "is best written, you think, amid groves and woods" (*inter nemora et lucos*), and this particular phrase is found in chapter 9 of the Dialogue. The clever French critic, Jules Janin, pronounced the work in question a *chef d'œuvre*, "revealing the highest genius," and could not understand how it could be doubted that Tacitus was the author. If so, it may be presumed to have been one of his earliest works. We gather from a passage in chapter 17, that the year in which the Dialogue or conversation was actually held was the sixth year of the reign of the Emperor Vespasian, or A D. 75. But it does not necessarily follow, as has been assumed, that it was written and published in the same year. It is at least quite possible that Tacitus, if he really was the author, may have taken notes of the conversation at the time, and have subsequently given them to the world, perhaps during the reigns of Nerva or Trajan, when he could have done so with safety. Domitian's age, as we know, was a very perilous one for certain kinds of literature.

The Dialogue is meant as an answer to a question which is put into the mouth of one Fabius Justus, a friend of the younger Pliny, and probably a professional rhetorician, a question which we may well suppose often occupied the thoughts of the speakers and men of letters of the day. "How is it," he asks, "that our own particular age is so destitute of the glory of eloquence, when former periods were so rich in it?" Tacitus replies that he should not care to give simply his own opinion on so great a subject, but that he is able to reproduce the substance of a discussion which he had had the good fortune to hear between some eminent men on this very topic. Of the personages of the Dialogue we know next to nothing. Four were present—Curiatius Maternus, Marcus Aper, Vipstanus Messala, and Julius Secundus. The last, of whom Quintilian says (x. 1, 120) that had he lived longer he would have been one of the most famous orators in the world (he was Quintilian's personal friend), takes but a very slight part in the conversation. Maternus had given up the pursuit of oratory for that of poetry, and had become a writer of tragedies. He is full of the praises of his art, which is, he argues, infinitely grander than that of the orator and the pleader of causes. He is probably mentioned by Dion Cassius, who speaks (67, 12) of a sophist, that is, a rhetoric-professor, whom Domitian put to death for his outspokenness against tyrants. Of Marcus Aper we can say nothing, but that he, like Secundus, was one of the great lights of the Roman bar. He is for oratory as against poetry, and he maintains that the eloquence of their own age was in its way quite as good as that of former days. Vipstanus Messala is not present at the beginning of the discussion; he comes in just as Maternus has concluded an enthusiastic encomium on the poet's life and pursuits. He was a man of whom Tacitus thought highly, and it is said of him in the History (iii. 9), that he was "the only man who had brought into the conflict between Vitellius and Vespasian an honest purpose." He was one of the adherents of the latter emperor. He is again mentioned in the History (iv. 42) as in a great crisis pleading most eloquently on behalf of his brother, Aquilius Regulus, the notorious *delator*, of whom the younger Pliny gives us a description in Epist. I., 5, one of his most amusing letters. It appears that he wrote memoirs of his time, which Tacitus used for his narrative of the civil wars in the History. In this Dialogue he is opposed to Aper, dwelling with admiration on the oratory of the old days of the republic, and vituperating that of his own age as a poor artificial product, the result of a depraved system of education, and of the extinction of all political ambition.

The subjects here discussed are of permanent interest. Aper pleads on behalf of his profession, its utility and substantial rewards, much as a barrister of our own day might do. He contrasts the great position and wealth won by a successful advocate, with the comparatively humble and obscure lot with which the poet must often rest content. The poet, indeed, at best, can hardly hope for much fame and popularity, or, if he really aspires to greatness, he must surrender himself wholly to his work, and turn his back on society and go into the solitude of fields and woods. Maternus in reply contends that this is a happier life than that of an overworked pleader, with all its harassing anxieties. Messala then joins in the conversation, and praises the orators of the past at the expense of the present, about whose inferiority he thinks there can be no question. In this view Secundus and Maternus concur. Aper vehemently denounces it, and criticises unfavourably several of the most famous orators of the republic, Cicero not excepted. After all, he says, how are you to draw a line between what is ancient and modern? People always praise the past, and disparage the present. Eloquence must change with the time, and adapt itself to altered conditions. If the eloquence of old days was more trenchant and vigorous, that of the present is more refined and elegant. People now would not tolerate the crudities and extravagances which disfigured the speeches of antiquity. However, both styles have their merits, and the right method is that of judicious combination. Aper fails to convince. Maternus assumes that the superiority of ancient oratory cannot be questioned, and he asks Messala to explain how it is that there has been such an evident decline of eloquence. Messala's reply, of which much is unfortunately lost, contrasts the education of the present with that of the past, and he argues that the methods in vogue in the schools of the rhetoric-professors are responsible for the inferior oratory of his own age. We have an amusing picture of the young barrister's defective and absurd training under these professors, from whom he learns only a certain art of declaiming glibly on some far-fetched and preposterous topic. The end of Messala's speech is lost; it would seem that he requested Maternus to give his ideas on the subject, and from this point to the conclusion of the Dialogue Maternus is the speaker. True eloquence, he maintains, can flourish only under a free government, and such a government, in fact, a republic, involves a certain amount of turbulence, which is really favourable to the orator. In such a state of things, political success is unattainable without eloquence. Indeed, the orator's art, if it is to flourish to perfection, needs the stimulus of strife and disorder, and can hardly find material for itself in quiet times and under a settled and established government. And so Athens was its home rather than Sparta. Maternus suggests that, if eloquence had declined, it was a cause for thankfulness, as such a fact implied that the conditions of life in their day were at all events better and happier than they had been amid the storms and convulsions of the "good old times." With these reflections the Dialogue concludes.

A DIALOGUE ON ORATORY.

YOU often ask me, Justus Fabius, how it is that while the genius and the fame of so many distinguished orators have shed a lustre on the past, our age is so forlorn and so destitute of the glory of eloquence that it scarce retains the very name of orator. That title indeed we apply only to the ancients, and the clever speakers of this day we call pleaders, advocates, counsellors, anything rather than orators. To answer this question of yours, to undertake the burden of so serious an inquiry, involving, as it must, a mean opinion either of our capacities, if we cannot reach the same standard, or of our tastes, if we have not the wish, is a task on which I should scarcely venture had I to give my own views instead of being able to reproduce a conversation among men, for our time, singularly eloquent, whom, when quite a youth, I heard discussing this very question. And so it is not ability, it is only memory and recollection which I require. I have to repeat now, with the same divisions and arguments, following closely the course of that discussion, those subtle reflections which I heard, powerfully expressed, from men of the highest eminence, each of whom assigned a different but plausible reason, CHAP I

CHAP. I. thereby displaying the peculiarities of his individual temper and genius Nor indeed did the opposite side lack an advocate, who, after much criticism and ridicule of old times, maintained the superiority of the eloquence of our own days to the great orators of the past.

CHAP II It was the day after Curiatius Maternus had given a reading of his Cato, by which it was said that he had irritated the feelings of certain great personages, because in the subject of his tragedy he had apparently forgotten himself and thought only of Cato. While all Rome was discussing the subject, he received a visit from Marcus Aper and Julius Secundus, then the most famous men of genius at our bar. Of both I was a studious hearer in court, and I also would follow them to their homes and when they appeared in public, from a singular zeal for my profession, and a youthful enthusiasm which urged me to listen diligently to their trivial talk, their more serious debates, and their private and esoteric discourse Yet many ill-naturedly thought that Secundus had no readiness of speech, and that Aper had won his reputation for eloquence by his cleverness and natural powers, more than by training and culture. As a fact, Secundus had a pure, terse, and a sufficiently fluent style, while Aper, who was imbued with learning of all kinds, pretended to despise the culture which he really possessed. He would have, so he must have thought, a greater reputation for industry and application, if it should appear that his genius did not depend on any supports from pursuits alien to his profession.

So we entered the study of Maternus, and found him seated with the very book which he had read the day before, in his hands Secundus began. Has the talk of ill-natured people no effect in deterring you, Maternus, from clinging to your Cato with its provocations? Or have you taken up the book to revise it more carefully, and, after striking out whatever has given a handle for a bad interpretation, will you publish, if not a better, at least a safer, Cato? CHAP. III

You shall read, was the answer, what Maternus owed it to himself to write, and all that you heard you will recognise again. Anything omitted in the Cato Thyestes shall supply in my next reading. This is a tragedy, the plan of which I have in my own mind arranged and formed. I am therefore bent on hurrying on the publication of the present book, that, as soon as my first work is off my hands, I may devote my whole soul to a fresh task.

It seems, said Aper, so far from these tragedies contenting you, that you have abandoned the study of the orator and pleader, and are giving all your time to Medea and now to Thyestes, although your friends, with their many causes, and your clients from the colonies, municipalities, and towns, are calling you to the courts. You could hardly answer their demands even if you had not imposed new work on yourself, the work of adding to the dramas of Greece a Domitius and a Cato, histories and names from our own Rome.

This severity of yours, replied Maternus, would be quite a blow to us, had not our controversy from CHAP. IV

CHAP V its frequency and familiarity become by this time almost a regular practice. You, in fact, never cease from abusing and inveighing against poets, and I, whom you reproach with neglect of my professional duties, every day undertake to plead against you in defence of poetry. So I am all the more delighted at the presence of a judge who will either forbid me for the future to write verses, or who will compel me by his additional authority to do what I have long desired, to give up the petty subleties of legal causes, at which I have toiled enough, and more than enough, and to cultivate a more sacred and more stately eloquence.

CHAP V For my part, said Secundus, before Aper refuses me as a judge, I will do as is usually done by upright and sensible judges, who excuse themselves in cases in which it is evident that one side has an undue influence with them. Who knows not that no one is nearer my heart from long friendship and uninterrupted intercourse than Saleius Bassus, an excellent man, as well as a most accomplished poet? Besides, if poetry is to be put on her defence, I know not a more influential defendant.

He may rest secure, said Aper, both Saleius Bassus himself, and anyone else who is devoted to the pursuit of poetry and the glory of song, if he has not the gift of pleading causes. But assuredly, as I have found an arbiter for this dispute, I will not allow Maternus to shelter himself behind a number of associates. I single him out for accusation before you on the ground that, though naturally fittest for that manly eloquence of the orator by which he might create and retain friendships, acquire connections, and attach the provinces, he is throwing away a pursuit than which it is impossible to imagine one in our state richer in advantages, more splendid in its prospects, more attractive in fame at home, more illustrious in celebrity throughout our whole empire and all the world. If, indeed, what is useful in life should be the aim of all our plans and actions, what can be safer than to practise an art armed with which a man can always bring aid to friends, succour to strangers, deliverance to the imperilled, while to malignant foes he is an actual fear and terror, himself the while secure and intrenched, so to say, within a power and a position of lasting strength? When we have a flow of prosperity, the efficacy and use of this art are seen in the help and protection of others; if, however, we hear the sound of danger to ourselves, the breast-plate and the sword are not, I am well assured, a stronger defence on the battle-field than eloquence is to a man amid the perils of a prosecution. It is both a shield and a weapon; you can use it alike for defence and attack, either before a judge, before the senate, or before the emperor. What but his eloquence did Eprius Marcellus oppose the other day to the senators in their fury? Armed with this, and consequently terrible, he baffled the sagacious but untrained wisdom of Helvidius Priscus, which knew nothing of such encounters. Of its usefulness I say no more. It is a point which I think my friend Maternus will be the last to dispute.

CHAP. VI. I pass now to the pleasure derived from the orator's eloquence. Its delights are enjoyed not for a single moment, but almost on every day and at every hour. To the mind of an educated gentleman, naturally fitted for worthy enjoyments, what can be more delightful than to see his house always thronged and crowded by gatherings of the most eminent men, and to know that the honour is paid not to his wealth, his childlessness, or his possession of some office, but to himself? Nay, more; the childless, the rich, and the powerful often go to one who is both young and poor, in order to intrust him with difficulties affecting themselves or their friends. Can there be any pleasure from boundless wealth and vast power equal to that of seeing men in years, and even in old age, men backed by the influence of the whole world, readily confessing, amid the utmost affluence of every kind, that they do not possess that which is the best of all? Again, look at the respectable citizens who escort the pleader to and from the court. Look at his appearance in public, and the respect shown him before the judges. What a delight it must be to rise and stand amid the hushed crowd, with every eye on him alone, the people assembling and gathering round him in a circle, and taking from the orator any emotion he has himself assumed. I am now reckoning the notorious joys of an orator, those which are open to the sight even of the uneducated; the more secret, known only to the advocate himself, are yet greater. If he produces a careful and well-prepared speech, there is a solidity and stedfastness in his satisfaction, just as there is in his style; if, again, he offers his audience, not without some tremblings at heart, the result of a fresh and sudden effort, his very anxiety enhances the joy of success, and ministers to his pleasure In fact, audacity at the moment, and rashness itself, have quite a peculiar sweetness. As with the earth, so with genius. Though time must be bestowed on the sowing and cultivation of some plants, yet those which grow spontaneously are the more pleasing. CHAP. VI

CHAP VII

To speak my own mind, I did not experience more joy on the day on which I was presented with the robe of a senator, or when, as a new man, born in a far from influential state, I was elected quæstor, or tribune, or prætor, than on those on which it was my privilege, considering the insignificance of my ability as a speaker, to defend a prisoner with success, to win a verdict in a cause before the Court of the Hundred, or to give the support of my advocacy in the emperor's presence to the great freedmen themselves, or to ministers of the crown. On such occasions I seem to rise above tribunates, prætorships, and consulships, and to possess that which, if it be not of natural growth, is not bestowed by mandate, nor comes through interest. Again, is there an accomplishment, the fame and glory of which are to be compared with the distinction of the orator, who is an illustrious man at Rome, not only with the busy class, intent on public affairs, but even with people of leisure, and with the young, those at least who have a right disposition and a worthy confidence in themselves? Whose name does the father din into his

CHAP. VII. children's ears before that of the orator? Whom, as he passes by, do the ignorant mob and the men with the tunic oftener speak of by name and point out with the finger? Strangers too and foreigners, having heard of him in their towns and colonies, as soon as they have arrived at Rome, ask for him and are eager, as it were, to recognise him.

CHAP. VIII. As for Marcellus Eprius, whom I have just mentioned, and Crispus Vibius (it is pleasanter to me to cite recent and modern examples than those of a distant and forgotten past), I would venture to argue that they are quite as great men in the remotest corners of the world as at Capua or Vercellae, where they are said to have been born. Nor do they owe this to the three hundred million sesterces of the one, although it may seem that they must thank their eloquence for having attained such wealth. Eloquence itself is the cause. Its inspiration and superhuman power have throughout all times shown by many an example what a height of fortune men have reached by the might of genius. But there are, as I said but now, instances close at hand, and we may know them, not by hearsay, but may see them with our eyes. The lower and meaner their birth, the more notorious the poverty and the straitened means amid which their life began, the more famous and brilliant are they as examples to show the efficacy of an orator's eloquence. Without the recommendation of birth, without the support of riches, neither of the two distinguished for virtue, one even despised for the appearance of his person, they have now for many years been the most powerful men in the state, and, as long as it suited them, they were the leaders of the bar. At this moment, as leading men in the emperor's friendship they carry all before them, and even the leading man himself of the State esteems and almost reverences them. Vespasian indeed, venerable in his old age and most tolerant of truth, knows well that while his other friends are dependent on what he has given them, and on what it is easy for him to heap and pile on others, Marcellus and Crispus, in becoming his friends, brought with them something which they had not received and which could not be received from a prince. Amid so much that is great, busts, inscriptions, and statues hold but a very poor place. Yet even these they do not disregard, and certainly not riches and affluence, which it is easier to find men denouncing than despising. It is these honours and splendours, aye and substantial wealth, that we see filling the homes of those who from early youth have given themselves to practice at the bar and to the study of oratory. CHAP. VIII

As for song and verse to which Maternus wishes to devote his whole life (for this was the starting-point of his entire argument), they bring no dignity to the author, nor do they improve his circumstances. Although your ears, Maternus, may loathe what I am about to say, I ask what good it is if Agamemnon or Jason speaks eloquently in your composition. Who the more goes back to his home saved from danger and bound to you? Our friend Saleius is an admirable poet, or, if the phrase be more CHAP. IX

CHAP. IX. complimentary, a most illustrious bard; but who walks by his side or attends his receptions or follows in his train? Why, if his friend or relative or even he himself stumbles into some troublesome affair, he will run to Secundus here, or to you, Maternus, not because you are a poet or that you may make verses for him; for verses come naturally to Bassus in his own home, and pretty and charming they are, though the result of them is that when, with the labour of a whole year, through entire days and the best part of the nights, he has hammered out, with the midnight oil, a single book, he is forced actually to beg and canvass for people who will condescend to be his hearers, and not even this without cost to himself. He gets the loan of a house, fits up a room, hires benches, and scatters programmes. Even if his reading is followed by a complete success, all the glory is, so to say, cut short in the bloom and the flower, and does not come to any real and substantial fruit. He carries away with him not a single friendship, not a single client, not an obligation that will abide in anyone's mind, only idle applause, meaningless acclamations and a fleeting delight. We lately praised Vespasian's bounty, in giving Bassus four thousand pounds, as something marvellous and splendid. It is no doubt a fine thing to win an emperor's favour by talent; but how much finer, if domestic circumstances so require, to cultivate oneself, to make one's own genius propitious, to fall back on one's own bounty. Consider too that a poet, if he wishes to work out and accomplish a worthy result, must leave the society of his friends, and the attractions of the capital; he must relinquish every other duty, and must, as poets themselves say, retire to woods and groves, in fact, into solitude. CHAP. IX

Nor again do even reputation and fame, the only object of their devotion, the sole reward of their labours, by their own confession, cling to the poet as much as to the orator; for indifferent poets are known to none, and the good but to a few When does the rumour of the very choicest readings penetrate every part of Rome, much less is talked of throughout our numerous provinces? How few, when they visit the capital from Spain or Asia, to say nothing of our Gallic neighbours, ask after Saleius Bassus! And indeed, if any one does ask after him, having once seen him, he passes on, and is satisfied, as if he had seen a picture or a statue I do not wish my remarks to be taken as implying that I would deter from poetry those to whom nature has denied the orator's talent, if only they can amuse their leisure and push themselves into fame by this branch of culture. For my part I hold all eloquence in its every variety something sacred and venerable, and I regard as preferable to all studies of other arts not merely your tragedian's buskin or the measures of heroic verse, but even the sweetness of the lyric ode, the playfulness of the elegy, the satire of the iambic, the wit of the epigram, and indeed any other form of eloquence. But it is with you, Maternus, that I am dealing; for, when your genius might carry you to the summit of eloquence, you prefer to wander from the path, CHAP X

CHAP. X and though sure to win the highest prize you stop short at meaner things Just as, if you had been born in Greece, where it is an honour to practise even the arts of the arena, and if the gods had given you the vigour and strength of Nicostratus, I should not suffer those giant arms meant by nature for combat to waste themselves on the light javelin or the throwing of the quoit, so now I summon you from the lecture-room and the theatre to the law court with its pleadings and its real battles. I do this the more because you cannot even fall back on the refuge which shelters many, the plea that the poet's pursuit is less liable to give offence than that of the orator. In truth, with you the ardour of a peculiarly noble nature bursts forth, and the offence you give is not for the sake of a friend, but, what is more dangerous, for the sake of Cato. Nor is this offending excused by the obligation of duty, or by the fidelity of an advocate, or by the impulse of a casual and sudden speech. You have, it seems, prepared your part in having chosen a character of note who would speak with authority. I foresee your possible answer. Hence, you will say, came the decisive approval; this is the style which the lecture-room chiefly praises, and which next becomes the world's talk Away then with the excuse of quiet and safety, when you are deliberately choosing a more doughty adversary For myself, let it be enough to take a side in the private disputes of our own time. In these, if at any time necessity has compelled us on behalf of an imperilled friend to offend the ears of the powerful, our loyalty must be approved, our liberty of speech condoned.

Aper having said this with his usual spirit and with vehemence of utterance, Maternus replied good-humouredly with something of a smile I was preparing to attack the orators at as great length as Aper had praised them, for I thought that he would leave his praises of them and go on to demolish poets and the pursuit of poetry, but he appeased me by a sort of stratagem, granting permission to those who cannot plead causes, to make verses. For myself, though I am perhaps able to accomplish and effect something in pleading causes, yet it was by the public reading of tragedies that I first began to enter the path of fame, when in Nero's time I broke the wicked power of Vatinius by which even the sanctities of culture were profaned, and if at this moment I possess any celebrity and distinction I maintain that it has been acquired more by the renown of my poems than of my speeches And so now I have resolved to throw off the yoke of my labours at the bar, and for trains of followers on my way to and from the court and for crowded receptions I crave no more than for the bronzes and busts which have invaded my house even against my will. For hitherto I have upheld my position and my safety better by integrity than by eloquence, and I am not afraid of having ever to say a word in the senate except to avert peril from another. CHAP XI

As to the woods and groves and that retirement which Aper denounced, they bring such delight to me that I count among the chief enjoyments of poetry the fact that it is composed not in the midst CHAP XII

CHAP. XII.

of bustle, or with a suitor sitting before one's door, or amid the wretchedness and tears of prisoners, but that the soul withdraws herself to abodes of purity and innocence, and enjoys her holy resting-place. Here eloquence had her earliest beginnings; here is her inmost shrine. In such guise and beauty did she first charm mortals, and steal into those virgin hearts which no vice had contaminated. Oracles spoke under these conditions. As for the present money-getting and blood-stained eloquence, its use is modern, its origin in corrupt manners, and, as you said, Aper, it is a device to serve as a weapon. But the happy golden age, to speak in our own poetic fashion, knew neither orators nor accusations, while it abounded in poets and bards, men who could sing of good deeds, but not defend evil actions. None enjoyed greater glory, or honours more august, first with the gods, whose answers they published, and at whose feasts they were present, as was commonly said, and then with the offspring of the gods and with sacred kings, among whom, so we have understood, was not a single pleader of causes, but an Orpheus, a Linus, and, if you care to dive into a remoter age, an Apollo himself. Or, if you think all this too fabulous and imaginary, at least you grant me that Homer has as much honour with posterity as Demosthenes, and that the fame of Euripides or Sophocles is bounded by a limit not narrower than that of Lysias or Hyperides. You will find in our own day more who disparage Cicero's than Virgil's glory. Nor is any production of Asinius or Messala so famous as Ovid's Medea or the Thyestes of Varius.

Look again at the poet's lot, with its delightful companionships. I should not be afraid of comparing it with the harassing and anxious life of the orator. Orators, it is true, have been raised to consulships by their contests and perils, but I prefer Virgil's serene, calm, and peaceful retirement, in which after all he was not without the favour of the divine Augustus, and fame among the people of Rome. We have the testimony of the letters of Augustus, the testimony too of the people themselves, who, on hearing in the theatre some of Virgil's verses, rose in a body and did homage to the poet, who happened to be present as a spectator, just as to Augustus himself. Even in our own day, Pomponius Secundus need not yield to Domitius Aper on the score of a dignified life or an enduring reputation. As for your Crispus and Marcellus, whom you hold up to me as examples, what is there in their lot to be coveted? Is it that they are in fear themselves, or are a fear to others? Is it that, while every day something is asked from them, those to whom they grant it feel indignant? Is it that, bound as they are by the chain of flattery, they are never thought servile enough by those who rule, or free enough by us? What is their power at its highest? Why, the freedmen usually have as much. For myself, as Virgil says, let "the sweet muses" lead me to their sacred retreats, and to their fountains far away from anxieties and cares, and the necessity of doing every day something repugnant to my heart. Let me no longer tremblingly experience the madness and perils of the forum, and the pallors of fame. Let me not be aroused by a

CHAP. XIII. tumult of morning visitors, or a freedman's panting haste, or, anxious about the future, have to make a will to secure my wealth. Let me not possess more than what I can leave to whom I please, whenever the day appointed by my own fates shall come; and let the statue over my tomb be not gloomy and scowling, but bright and laurel-crowned. As for my memory, let there be no resolutions in the senate, or petitions to the emperor.

CHAP. XIV. Excited and, I may say, full of enthusiasm, Maternus had hardly finished when Vipstanus Messala entered his room, and, from the earnest expression on each face, he conjectured that their conversation was unusually serious. Have I, he asked, come among you unseasonably, while you are engaged in private deliberation, or the preparation of some case?

By no means, by no means, said Secundus. Indeed I could wish you had come sooner, for you would have been delighted with the very elaborate arguments of our friend Aper, in which he urged Maternus to apply all his ability and industry to the pleading of causes, and then too with Maternus's apology for his poems in a lively speech, which, as suited a poet's defence, was uncommonly spirited, and more like poetry than oratory.

For my part, he replied, I should have been infinitely charmed by the discourse, and I am delighted to find that you excellent men, the orators of our age, instead of exercising your talents simply on law-business and rhetorical studies, also engage in discussions which not only strengthen the intellect but also draw from learning and from letters a pleasure most exquisite both to you who discuss such subjects and to those too whose ears your words may reach. Hence the world, I see, is as much pleased with you, Secundus, for having by your life of Julius Asiaticus given it the promise of more such books, as it is with Aper for having not yet retired from the disputes of the schools, and for choosing to employ his leisure after the fashion of modern rhetoricians rather than of the old orators. CHAP XIV

Upon this Aper replied, You still persist, Messala, in admiring only what is old and antique and in sneering at and disparaging the culture of our own day. I have often heard this sort of talk from you, when, forgetting the eloquence of yourself and your brother, you argued that nobody in this age is an orator. And you did this, I believe, with the more audacity because you were not afraid of a reputation for ill-nature, seeing that the glory which others concede to you, you deny to yourself. I feel no penitence, said Messala, for such talk, nor do I believe that Secundus or Maternus or you yourself, Aper, think differently, though now and then you argue for the opposite view. I could wish that one of you were prevailed on to investigate and describe to us the reasons of this vast difference. I often inquire into them by myself. That which consoles some minds, to me increases the difficulty. For I perceive that even with the Greeks it has happened that there is a greater distance between Aeschines and Demosthenes on the one hand, and your friend Nicetes or any other orator CHAP XV

CHAP XV who shakes Ephesus or Mitylene with a chorus of rhetoricians and their noisy applause, on the other, than that which separates Afer, Africanus, or yourselves from Cicero or Asinius.

CHAP XVI The question you have raised, said Secundus, is a great one and quite worthy of discussion. But who has a better claim to unravel it than yourself, you who to profound learning and transcendent ability have added reflection and study?

I will open my mind to you, replied Messala, if first I can prevail on you to give me your assistance in our discussion. I can answer for two of us, said Maternus; Secundus and myself will take the part which we understand you have not so much omitted as left to us. Aper usually dissents, as you have just said, and he has clearly for some time been girding himself for the attack, and cannot bear with patience our union on behalf of the merits of the ancients.

Assuredly, said Aper, I will not allow our age to be condemned, unheard and undefended, by this conspiracy of yours. First, however, I will ask you whom you call ancients, or what period of orators you limit by your definition? When I hear of ancients, I understand men of the past, born ages ago; I have in my eye Ulysses and Nestor, whose time is about thirteen hundred years before our day. But you bring forward Demosthenes and Hyperides who flourished, as we know, in the period of Philip and Alexander, a period, however, which they both outlived. Hence we see that not much more than four hundred years has intervened between our own era and that of Demosthenes.

If you measure this space of time by the frailty of human life, it perhaps seems long; if by the course of ages and by the thought of this boundless universe, it is extremely short and is very near us. For indeed, if, as Cicero says in his Hortensius, the great and the true year is that in which the position of the heavens and of the stars at any particular moment recurs, and if that year embraces twelve thousand nine hundred and ninety four of what we call years, then your Demosthenes, whom you represent as so old and ancient, began his existence not only in the same year, but almost in the same month as ourselves. CHAP XVI

But I pass to the Latin orators. Among them, it is not, I imagine, Menenius Agrippa, who may seem ancient, whom you usually prefer to the speakers of our day, but Cicero, Caelius, Calvus, Brutus, Asinius, Messala. Why you assign them to antiquity rather than to our own times, I do not see. With respect to Cicero himself, it was in the consulship of Hirtius and Pansa, as his freedman Tiro has stated, on the 5th of December, that he was slain. In that same year the Divine Augustus elected himself and Quintus Pedius consuls in the room of Pansa and Hirtius. Fix at fifty-six years the subsequent rule of the Divine Augustus over the state; add Tiberius's three-and-twenty years, the four years or less of Caius, the twenty-eight years of Claudius and Nero, the one memorable long year of Galba, Otho, and Vitellius, and the now six years of the present happy reign, during which Vespasian has been fostering the public weal, and the result is that from Cicero's death to our CHAP XVII

CHAP. XVII. day is a hundred and twenty years, one man's life-time. For I saw myself an old man in Britain who declared that he was present at the battle in which they strove to drive and beat back from their shores the arms of Cæsar when he attacked their island. So, had this man who encountered Cæsar in the field, been brought to Rome either as a prisoner, or by his own choice or by some destiny, he might have heard Cæsar himself and Cicero, and also have been present at our own speeches. At the last largess of the Emperor you saw yourselves several old men who told you that they had actually shared once and again in the gifts of the divine Augustus. Hence we infer that they might have heard both Corvinus and Asinius Corvinus indeed lived on to the middle of the reign of Augustus, Asinius almost to its close. You must not then divide the age, and habitually describe as old and ancient orators those with whom the ears of the self-same men might have made acquaintance, and whom they might, so to say, have linked and coupled together.

CHAP. XVIII. I have made these preliminary remarks to show that any credit reflected on the age by the fame and renown of these orators is common property, and is in fact more closely connected with us than with Servius Galba or Caius Carbo, and others whom we may rightly call "ancients." These indeed are rough, unpolished, awkward, and ungainly, and I wish that your favourite Calvus or Caelius or even Cicero had in no respect imitated them. I really mean now to deal with the subject more boldly and confidently, but I must first observe that the types and varieties of eloquence change with the age. Thus Caius Gracchus compared with the elder Cato is full and copious; Crassus compared with Gracchus is polished and ornate; Cicero compared with either is lucid, graceful, and lofty; Corvinus again is softer and sweeter and more finished in his phrases than Cicero. I do not ask who is the best speaker. Meantime I am content to have proved that eloquence has more than one face, and even in those whom you call ancients several varieties are to be discovered. Nor does it at once follow that difference implies inferiority. It is the fault of envious human nature that the old is always the object of praise, the present of contempt. Can we doubt that there were found critics who admired Appius Caecus more than Cato? We know that even Cicero was not without his disparagers, who thought him inflated, turgid, not concise enough, but unduly diffuse and luxuriant, in short anything but Attic. You have read of course the letters of Calvus and Brutus to Cicero, and from these it is easy to perceive that in Cicero's opinion Calvus was bloodless and attenuated, Brutus slovenly and lax. Cicero again was slightingly spoken of by Calvus as loose and nerveless, and by Brutus, to use his own words, as "languid and effeminate." If you ask me, I think they all said what was true. But I shall come to them separately after a while; now I have to deal with them collectively. CHAP XVIII.

While indeed the admirers of the ancients fix as the boundary, so to say, of antiquity, the period up to Cassius Severus who was the first, they assert, to CHAP. XIX.

CHAP XIX

deviate from the old and plain path of the speaker, I maintain that it was not from poverty of genius or ignorance of letters that he adopted his well known style, but from preference and intellectual conviction. He saw, in fact, that, as I was just now saying, the character and type of oratory must change with the circumstances of the age and an altered taste in the popular ear. The people of the past, ignorant and uncultured as they were, patiently endured the length of a very confused speech, and it was actually to the speaker's credit, if he took up one of their days by his speech-making Then too they highly esteemed long preparatory introductions, narratives told from a remote beginning, a multitude of divisions ostentatiously paraded, proofs in a thousand links, and all the other directions prescribed in those driest of treatises by Hermagoras and Apollodorus Any one who was supposed to have caught a scent of philosophy, and who introduced some philosophical commonplace into his speech, was praised up to the skies. And no wonder; for this was new and unfamiliar, and even of the orators but very few had studied the rules of rhetoricians or the dogmas of philosophers. But now that all these are common property and that there is scarce a bystander in the throng who, if not fully instructed, has not at least been initiated into the rudiments of culture, eloquence must resort to new and skilfully chosen paths, in order that the orator may avoid offence to the fastidious ear, at any rate before judges who decide by power and authority, not by law and precedent, who fix the speaker's time, instead of leaving it to himself, and, so far from thinking that they ought to wait till he chooses to speak on the matter in question, continually remind him of it and recall him to it when he wanders, protesting that they are in a hurry CHAP XIX.

Who will now tolerate an advocate who begins by speaking of the feebleness of his constitution, as is usual in the openings of Corvinus? Who will sit out the five books against Verres? Who will endure those huge volumes, on a legal plea or form, which we have read in the speeches for Marcus Tullius and Aulus Caecina? In our day the judge anticipates the speaker, and unless he is charmed and imposed on by the train of arguments, or the brilliancy of the thoughts, or the grace and elegance of the descriptive sketches, he is deaf to his eloquence. Even the mob of bystanders, and the chance listeners who flock in, now usually require brightness and beauty in a speech, and they no more endure in the law-court the harshness and roughness of antiquity, than they would an actor on the stage who chose to reproduce the gestures of Roscius or Ambivius. So again the young, those whose studies are on the anvil, who go after the orators with a view to their own progress, are anxious not merely to hear but also to carry back home some brilliant passage worthy of remembrance. They tell it one to another, and often mention it in letters to their colonies and provinces, whether it is a reflection lighted up by a neat and pithy phrase, or a passage bright with choice and poetic ornament. For we now expect from a speaker even poetic beauty, not indeed soiled with CHAP. XX.

CHAP. XX. the old rust of Accius or Pacuvius, but such as is produced from the sacred treasures of Horace, Virgil, and Lucan. Thus the age of our orators, in conforming itself to the ear and the taste of such a class, has advanced in beauty and ornateness. Nor does it follow that our speeches are less successful because they bring pleasure to the ears of those who have to decide. What if you were to assume that the temples of the present day are weaker, because, instead of being built of rough blocks and ill-shaped tiles, they shine with marble and glitter with gold?

CHAP. XXI. I will frankly admit to you that I can hardly keep from laughing at some of the ancients, and from falling asleep at others. I do not single out any of the common herd, as Canutius, or Arrius, and others in the same sick-room, so to say, who are content with mere skin and bones. Even Calvus, although he has left, I think, one-and-twenty volumes, scarcely satisfies me in one or two short speeches. The rest of the world, I see, does not differ from my opinion about him; for how few read his speeches against Asitius or Drusus! Certainly his impeachment of Vatinius, as it is entitled, is in the hands of students, especially the second of the orations. This, indeed, has a finish about the phrases and the periods, and suits the ear of the critic, whence you may infer that even Calvus understood what a better style is, but that he lacked genius and power rather than the will to speak with more dignity and grace. What again from the speeches of Caelius do we admire? Why, we like of these the whole, or at least parts, in which we recognise the polish and elevation of our own day; but, as for those mean expressions, those gaps in the structure of the sentences, and uncouth sentiments, they savour of antiquity. No one, I suppose, is so thoroughly antique as to praise Caelius simply on the side of his antiqueness. We may, indeed, make allowance for Caius Julius Cæsar, on account of his vast schemes and many occupations, for having achieved less in eloquence than his divine genius demanded from him, and leave him indeed, just as we leave Brutus to his philosophy. Undoubtedly in his speeches he fell short of his reputation, even by the admission of his admirers. I hardly suppose that any one reads Cæsar's speech for Decius the Samnite, or that of Brutus for King Deiotarus, or other works equally dull and cold, unless it is some one who also admires their poems. For they did write poems, and sent them to libraries, with no better success than Cicero, but with better luck, because fewer people know that they wrote them.

CHAP XXI

Asinius too, though born in a time nearer our own, seems to have studied with the Menenii and Appii. At any rate he imitated Pacuvius and Accius, not only in his tragedies but also in his speeches; he is so harsh and dry. Style, like the human body, is then specially beautiful when, so to say, the veins are not prominent, and the bones cannot be counted, but when a healthy and sound blood fills the limbs, and shows itself in the muscles, and the very sinews become beautiful under a ruddy glow and graceful outline. I will not attack Corvinus, for it was not indeed his own fault that he did not exhibit the

CHAP. XXI. luxuriance and brightness of our own day. Rather let us note how far the vigour of his intellect or of his imagination satisfied his critical faculty.

CHAP. XXII. I come now to Cicero. He had the same battle with his contemporaries which I have with you. They admired the ancients; he preferred the eloquence of his own time. It was in taste more than anything else that he was superior to the orators of that age. In fact, he was the first who gave a finish to oratory, the first who applied a principle of selection to words, and art to composition. He tried his skill at beautiful passages, and invented certain arrangements of the sentence, at least in those speeches which he composed when old and near the close of life, that is when he had made more progress, and had learnt by practice and by many a trial, what was the best style of speaking. As for his early speeches, they are not free from the faults of antiquity. He is tedious in his introductions, lengthy in his narrations, careless about digressions; he is slow to rouse himself, and seldom warms to his subject, and only an idea here and there is brought to a fitting and a brilliant close. There is nothing which you can pick out or quote, and the style is like a rough building, the wall of which indeed is strong and lasting, but not particularly polished and bright. Now I would have an orator, like a rich and grand householder, not merely be sheltered by a roof sufficient to keep off rain and wind, but by one to delight the sight and the eye; not merely be provided with such furniture as is enough for necessary purposes, but also possess among his treasures gold and jewels, so that he may find a frequent pleasure in handling them and gazing on them. On the other hand, some things should be kept at a distance as being now obsolete and ill-savoured. There should be no phrase stained, so to speak, with rust; no ideas should be expressed in halting and languid periods after the fashion of chronicles. The orator must shun an offensive and tasteless scurrility; he must vary the structure of his sentences and not end all his clauses in one and the same way. CHAP. XXII.

Phrases like "Fortune's wheel" and "Verrine soup," I do not care to ridicule, or that stock ending of every third clause in all Cicero's speeches, "it would seem to be," brought in as the close of a period. I have mentioned them with reluctance, omitting several, although they are the sole peculiarities admired and imitated by those who call themselves orators of the old school. I will not name any one, as I think it enough to have pointed at a class. Still, you have before your eyes men who read Lucilius rather than Horace, and Lucretius rather than Virgil, who have a mean opinion of the eloquence of Aufidius Bassus, and Servilius Nonianus compared with that of Sisenna or Varro, and who despise and loathe the treatises of our modern rhetoricians, while those of Calvus are their admiration. When these men prose in the old style before the judges, they have neither select listeners nor a popular audience; in short the client himself hardly endures them. They are dismal and uncouth, and the very soundness of which they boast, is the result not so much of real vigour as of fasting. Even CHAP. XXIII.

CHAP. XXIII.

as to health of body, physicians are not satisfied with that which is attained at the cost of mental worry. It is a small matter not to be ill; I like a man to be robust and hearty and full of life. If soundness is all that you can praise him for, he is not very far from being an invalid. Be it yours, my eloquent friends, to grace our age to the best of your ability, as in fact you are doing, with the noblest style of oratory. You, Messala, imitate, I observe, the choicest beauties of the ancients. And you, Maternus and Secundus, combine charm and finish of expression with weight of thought. There is discrimination in the phrases you invent, order in the treatment of your subject, fullness, when the case demands it, conciseness, when it is possible, elegance in your style, and perspicuity in every sentence. You can express passion, and yet control an orator's licence. And so, although ill-nature and envy may have stood in the way of our good opinions, posterity will speak the truth concerning you.

CHAP. XXIV.

Aper having finished speaking, Maternus said, You recognise, do you not, our friend Aper's force and passion? With what a torrent, what a rush of eloquence has he been defending our age? How full and varied was his tirade against the ancients! What ability and spirit, what learning and skill too did he show in borrowing from the very men themselves the weapons with which he forthwith proceeded to attack them! Still, as to your promise, Messala, there must for all this be no change. We neither want a defence of the ancients, nor do we compare any of ourselves, though we have just heard our own praises, with those whom Aper has denounced. Aper himself thinks otherwise; he merely followed an old practice much in vogue with your philosophical school of assuming the part of an opponent Give us then not a panegyric on the ancients (their own fame is a sufficient panegyric) but tell us plainly the reasons why with us there has been such a falling off from their eloquence, the more marked as dates have proved that from the death of Cicero to this present day is but a hundred and twenty years. CHAP. XXIV

Messala replied, I will take the line you have prescribed for me. Certainly I need not argue long against Aper, who began by raising what I think a controversy about a name, implying that it is not correct to call ancients those whom we all know to have lived a hundred years ago I am not fighting about a word. Let him call them ancients or elders or any other name he prefers, provided only we have the admission that the eloquence of that age exceeded ours If again he freely admits that even in the same, much more in different periods, there were many varieties of oratory, against this part too of his argument I say nothing. I maintain, however, that just as among Attic orators we give the first place to Demosthenes and assign the next to Aeschines, Hyperides, Lysias and Lycurgus, while all agree in regarding this as pre-eminently the age of speakers, so among ourselves Cicero indeed was superior to all the eloquent men of his day, though Calvus, Asinius, Cæsar, Caelius, and Brutus may claim the right of being preferred to those who preceded and who CHAP XXV

CHAP. XXV. followed them. It matters nothing that they differ in special points, seeing that they are generically alike. Calvus is the more terse, Asinius has the finer rhythm, Cæsar greater brilliancy, Caelius is the more caustic, Brutus the more earnest, Cicero the more impassioned, the richer and more forcible. Still about them all there is the same healthy tone of eloquence. Take into your hand the works of all alike and you see that amid wide differences of genius, there is a resemblance and affinity of intellect and moral purpose. Grant that they disparaged each other (and certainly there are some passages in their letters which show mutual ill-will), still this is the failing, not of the orator, but of the man. Calvus, Asinius, Cicero himself, I presume, were apt to be envious and ill-natured, and to have the other faults of human infirmity. Brutus alone of the number in my opinion laid open the convictions of his heart frankly and ingenuously, without ill-will or envy. Is it possible that he envied Cicero, when he seems not to have envied even Cæsar? As to Servius Galba, and Caius Laelius, and others of the ancients whom Aper has persistently assailed, he must not expect me to defend them, for I admit that their eloquence, being yet in its infancy and imperfectly developed, had certain defects.

CHAP. XXVI. After all, if I must put on one side the highest and most perfect type of eloquence and select a style, I should certainly prefer the vehemence of Caius Gracchus or the sobriety of Lucius Crassus to the curls of Maecenas or the jingles of Gallio: so much better is it for an orator to wear a rough dress than to glitter in many-coloured and meretricious attire. Indeed, neither for an orator or even a man is that style becoming which is adopted by many of the speakers of our age, and which, with its idle redundancy of words, its meaningless periods and licence of expression, imitates the art of the actor. Shocking as it ought to be to our ears, it is a fact that fame, glory, and genius are sacrificed by many to the boast that their compositions are given with the tones of the singer, the gestures of the dancer. Hence the exclamation, which, though often heard, is a shame and an absurdity, that our orators speak prettily and our actors dance eloquently. For myself I would not deny that Cassius Severus, the only speaker whom Aper ventured to name, may, if compared with his successors, be called an orator, although in many of his works he shows more violence than vigour. The first to despise arrangement, to cast off propriety and delicacy of expression, confused by the very weapons he employs, and often stumbling in his eagerness to strike, he wrangles rather than fights. Still, as I have said, compared with his successors, he is far superior to all in the variety of his learning, the charm of his wit, and the solidity of his very strength. Not one of them has Aper had the courage to mention, and, so to say, to bring into the field. When he had censured Asinius, Caelius, and Calvus, I expected that he would show us a host of others, and name more, or at least as many who might be pitted man by man against Cicero, Cæsar, and the rest. As it is, he has contented himself with singling

CHAP. XXVI.

CHAP. XXVI. out for disparagement some ancient orators, and has not dared to praise any of their successors, except generally and in terms common to all, fearing, I suppose, that he would offend many, if he selected a few. For there is scarce one of our rhetoricians who does not rejoice in his conviction that he is to be ranked before Cicero, but unquestionably second to Gabinianus.

CHAP. XXVII. For my own part I shall not scruple to mention men by name, that, with examples before us, we may the more easily perceive the successive steps of the ruin and decay of eloquence.

Maternus here interrupted him. Rather prepare yourself to fulfil your promise. We do not want proof of the superior eloquence of the ancients; as far as I am concerned, it is admitted. We are inquiring into the causes, and these you told us but now you had been in the habit of discussing, when you were less excited and were not raving against the eloquence of our age, just before Aper offended you by attacking your ancestors.

I was not offended, replied Messala, by our friend Aper's argument, nor again will you have a right to be offended, if any remark of mine happens to grate on your ears, for you know that it is a rule in these discussions that we may speak out our convictions without impairing mutual good-will.

Proceed, said Maturnus As you are speaking of the ancients, avail yourself of ancient freedom, from which we have fallen away even yet more than from eloquence.

CHAP. XXVIII. Messala continued. Far from obscure are the

causes which you seek. Neither to yourself or to our friends, Secundus and Aper, are they unknown, though you assign me the part of speaking out before you what we all think. Who does not know that eloquence and all other arts have declined from their ancient glory, not from dearth of men, but from the indolence of the young, the carelessness of parents, the ignorance of teachers, and neglect of the old discipline? The evils which first began in Rome soon spread through Italy, and are now diffusing themselves into the provinces. But your provincial affairs are best known to yourselves. I shall speak of Rome, and of those native and home-bred vices which take hold of us as soon as we are born, and multiply with every stage of life, when I have first said a few words on the strict discipline of our ancestors in the education and training of children. Every citizen's son, the child of a chaste mother, was from the beginning reared, not in the chamber of a purchased nurse, but in that mother's bosom and embrace, and it was her special glory to study her home and devote herself to her children. It was usual to select an elderly kinswoman of approved and esteemed character to have the entire charge of all the children of the household. In her presence it was the last offence to utter an unseemly word or to do a disgraceful act. With scrupulous piety and modesty she regulated not only the boy's studies and occupations, but even his recreations and games. Thus it was, as tradition says, that the mothers of the Gracchi, of Cæsar, of Augustus, Cornelia, Aurelia, Atia, directed their children's education and reared the

CHAP. XXVIII. greatest of sons. The strictness of the discipline tended to form in each case a pure and virtuous nature which no vices could warp, and which would at once with the whole heart seize on every noble lesson. Whatever its bias, whether to the soldier's or the lawyer's art, or to the study of eloquence, it would make that its sole aim, and imbibe it in its fullness.

CHAP. XXIX. But in our day we entrust the infant to a little Greek servant-girl who is attended by one or two, commonly the worst of all the slaves, creatures utterly unfit for any important work. Their stories and their prejudices from the very first fill the child's tender and uninstructed mind. No one in the whole house cares what he says or does before his infant master. Even parents themselves familiarise their little ones, not with virtue and modesty, but with jesting and glib talk, which lead on by degrees to shamelessness and to contempt for themselves as well as for others. Really I think that the characteristic and peculiar vices of this city, a liking for actors and a passion for gladiators and horses, are all but conceived in the mother's womb. When these occupy and possess the mind, how little room has it left for worthy attainments! Few indeed are to be found who talk of any other subjects in their homes, and whenever we enter a class-room, what else is the conversation of the youths. Even with the teachers, these are the more frequent topics of talk with their scholars. In fact, they draw pupils, not by strictness of discipline or by giving proof of ability, but by assiduous court and cunning tricks of flattery.

I say nothing about the learners' first rudiments. Even with these little pains are taken, and on the reading of authors, on the study of antiquity and a knowledge of facts, of men and of periods, by no means enough labour is bestowed. It is rhetoricians, as they are called, who are in request. When this profession was first introduced into our city, and how little esteem it had among our ancestors, I am now about to explain; but I will first recall your attention to the training which we have been told was practised by those orators whose infinite industry, daily study and incessant application to every branch of learning are seen in the contents of their own books. You are doubtless familiar with Cicero's book, called Brutus. In the latter part of it (the first gives an account of the ancient orators) he relates his own beginnings, his progress, and the growth, so to say, of his eloquence. He tells us that he learnt the civil law under Quintus Mucius, and that he thoroughly imbibed every branch of philosophy under Philo of the Academy and under Diodotus the Stoic; that not content with the teachers under whom he had had the opportunity of studying at Rome, he travelled through Achaia and Asia Minor so as to embrace every variety of every learned pursuit. Hence we really find in Cicero's works that he was not deficient in the knowledge of geometry, music, grammar, or, in short, any liberal accomplishment. The subtleties of logic, the useful lessons of ethical science, the movements and causes of the universe, were alike known to him. The truth indeed is this, my excellent friends, that Cicero's wonderful eloquence wells up and overflows out of a store of CHAP XXX

CHAP. XXX. erudition, a multitude of accomplishments, and a knowledge that was universal. The strength and power of oratory, unlike all other arts, is not confined within narrow and straitened limits, but the orator is he who can speak on every question with grace, elegance, and persuasiveness, suitably to the dignity of his subject, the requirements of the occasion, and the taste of his audience.

CHAP. XXXI. Such was the conviction of the ancients, and to produce this result they were aware that it was necessary not only to declaim in the schools of rhetoricians, or to exercise the tongue and the voice in fictitious controversies quite remote from reality, but also to imbue the mind with those studies which treat of good and evil, of honour and dishonour, of right and wrong. All this, indeed, is the subject-matter of the orator's speeches. Equity in the law-court, honour in the council-chamber, are our usual topics of discussion. Still, these often pass into each other, and no one can speak on them with fulness, variety, and elegance but he who has studied human nature, the power of virtue, the depravity of vice, and the conception of those things which can be classed neither among virtues nor vices. These are the sources whence flows the greater ease with which he who knows what anger is, rouses or soothes the anger of a judge, the readier power with which he moves to pity who knows what pity is, and what emotions of the soul excite it. An orator practised in such arts and exercises, whether he has to address the angry, the biassed, the envious, the sorrowful, or the trembling, will understand different mental conditions, apply his skill, adapt his style, and have every instrument of his craft in readiness, or in reserve for every occasion. Some there are whose assent is more secured by an incisive and terse style, in which each inference is rapidly drawn. With such, it will be an advantage to have studied logic. Others are more attracted by a diffuse and smoothly flowing speech, appealing to the common sentiments of humanity. To impress such we must borrow from the Peripatetics commonplaces suited and ready prepared for every discussion. The Academy will give us combativeness, Plato, sublimity, Xenophon, sweetness. Nor will it be unseemly in an orator to adopt even certain exclamations of honest emotion, from Epicurus and Metrodorus, and to use them as occasion requires. It is not a philosopher after the Stoic school whom we are forming, but one who ought to imbibe thoroughly some studies, and to have a taste of all. Accordingly, knowledge of the civil law was included in the training of the ancient orators, and they also imbued their minds with grammar, music, and geometry. In truth, in very many, I may say in all cases, acquaintance with law is desirable, and in several this last-mentioned knowledge is a necessity. CHAP XXXI

Let no one reply that it is enough for us to learn, as occasion requires, some single and detached subject. In the first place we use our own property in one way, a loan in another, and there is evidently a wide difference between possessing what one exhibits CHAP XXXII

CHAP XXXII. and borrowing it. Next, the very knowledge of many subjects sits gracefully on us, even when we are otherwise engaged, and makes itself visible and conspicuous where you would least expect it. Even the average citizen, and not only the learned and critical hearer, perceives it, and forthwith showers his praises in the acknowledgment that the man has been a genuine student, has gone through every branch of eloquence, and is, in short, an orator. And I maintain that the only orator is, and ever has been, one who, like a soldier equipped at all points going to the battle-field, enters the forum armed with every learned accomplishment.

All this is so neglected by the speakers of our time that we detect in their pleadings the style of every-day conversation, and unseemly and shameful deficiencies. They are ignorant of the laws, they do not understand the senate's decrees, they actually scoff at the civil law, while they quite dread the study of philosophy, and the opinions of the learned; and eloquence, banished, so to say, from her proper realm, is dragged down by them into utter poverty of thought and constrained periods. Thus she who, once mistress of all the arts, held sway with a glorious retinue over our souls, now clipped and shorn, without state, without honour, I had almost said without her freedom, is studied as one of the meanest handicrafts. This then I believe to be the first and chief cause of so marked a falling off among us from the eloquence of the old orators. If witnesses are wanted, whom shall I name in preference to Demosthenes among the Greeks, who is said by tradition to have been a most attentive hearer of Plato? Cicero too tells us, I think, in these very words, that whatever he had achieved in eloquence he had gained, not from rhetoricians, but in the walks of the Academy. There are other causes, some of them great and important, which it is for you in fairness to explain, as I have now done my part, and, after my usual way, have offended pretty many persons who, if they happen to hear all this, will, I am sure, say that, in praising an acquaintance with law and philosophy as a necessity for an orator, I have been applauding my own follies. CHAP XXXII

For myself, replied Maternus, I do not think that you have completed the task which you undertook. Far from it. You have, I think, only made a beginning, and indicated, so to say, its traces and outlines. You have indeed described to us the usual equipment of the ancient orators, and pointed out the contrast presented by our idleness and ignorance to their very diligent and fruitful studies. I want to hear the rest. Having learnt from you what they knew, with which we are unacquainted, I wish also to be told the process of training by which, when mere lads, and when about to enter the forum, they used to strengthen and nourish their intellects. For you will not, I imagine, deny that eloquence depends much less on art and theory than on capacity and practice, and our friends here seem by their looks to think the same. CHAP XXXIII

Aper and Secundus having assented, Messala, so to say, began afresh. As I have, it seems, explained

CHAP. XXXIII to your satisfaction the first elements and the germs of ancient eloquence in showing you the studies in which the orator of antiquity was formed and educated, I will now discuss the process of his training However, even the studies themselves involve a training, and no one can acquire such profound and varied knowledge without adding practice to theory, fluency to practice, and eloquence itself to fluency. Hence we infer that the method of acquiring what you mean to produce publicly, and of so producing what you have acquired, is one and the same. Still, if any one thinks this somewhat obscure, and distinguishes broadly between theory and practice, he will at least allow that a mind thoroughly furnished and imbued with such studies will enter with a far better preparation on the kinds of practice which seem specially appropriate to the orator.

CHAP. XXXIV. It was accordingly usual with our ancestors, when a lad was being prepared for public speaking, as soon as he was fully trained by home discipline, and his mind was stored with culture, to have him taken by his father, or his relatives to the orator who held the highest rank in the state. The boy used to accompany and attend him, and be present at all his speeches, alike in the law-court and the assembly, and thus he picked up the art of repartee, and became habituated to the strife of words, and indeed, I may almost say, learnt how to fight in battle. Thereby young men acquired from the first great experience and confidence, and a very large stock of discrimination, for they were studying in broad daylight, in the very thick of the conflict, where no one can say anything foolish or self-contradictory without its being refuted by the judge, or ridiculed by the opponent, or, last of all, repudiated by the very counsel with him. Thus from the beginning they were imbued with true and genuine eloquence, and, although they attached themselves to one pleader, still they became acquainted with all advocates of their own standing in a multitude of cases before the courts. They had too abundant experience of the popular ear in all its greatest varieties, and with this they could easily ascertain what was liked or disapproved in each speaker. Thus they were not in want of a teacher of the very best and choicest kind, who could show them eloquence in her true features, not in a mere resemblance; nor did they lack opponents and rivals, who fought with actual steel, not with a wooden sword, and the audience too was always crowded, always changing, made up of unfriendly as well as of admiring critics, so that neither success nor failure could be disguised. You know, of course, that eloquence wins its great and enduring fame quite as much from the benches of our opponents as from those of our friends; nay, more, its rise from that quarter is steadier, and its growth surer. Undoubtedly it was under such teachers that the youth of whom I am speaking, the disciple of orators, the listener in the forum, the student in the law-courts, was trained and practised by the experiences of others. The laws he learnt by daily hearing; the faces of the judges were familiar to him; the ways of popular assemblies were continually before his eyes; he

CHAP. XXXIV. had frequent experience of the ear of the people, and whether he undertook a prosecution or a defence, he was at once singly and alone equal to any case. We still read with admiration the speeches in which Lucius Crassus in his nineteenth, Cæsar and Asinius Pollio in their twenty-first year, Calvus, when very little older, denounced, respectively, Carbo, Dolabella, Cato, and Vatinius

CHAP. XXXV. But in these days we have our youths taken to the professors' theatre, the rhetoricians, as we call them. The class made its appearance a little before Cicero's time, and was not liked by our ancestors, as is evident from the fact that, when Crassus and Domitius were censors, they were ordered, as Cicero says, to close "the school of impudence." However, as I was just saying, the boys are taken to schools in which it is hard to tell whether the place itself, or their fellow-scholars, or the character of their studies, do their minds most harm. As for the place, there is no such thing as reverence, for no one enters it who is not as ignorant as the rest. As for the scholars, there can be no improvement, when boys and striplings with equal assurance address, and are addressed by, other boys and striplings. As for the mental exercises themselves, they are the reverse of beneficial. Two kinds of subject-matter are dealt with before the rhetoricians, the persuasive and the controversial. The persuasive, as being comparatively easy and requiring less skill, is given to boys. The controversial is assigned to riper scholars, and, good heavens! what strange and astonishing productions

CHAP. XXXV.

are the result! It comes to pass that subjects remote from all reality are actually used for declamation. Thus the reward of a tyrannicide, or the choice of an outraged maiden, or a remedy for a pestilence, or a mother's incest, anything, in short, daily discussed in our schools, never, or but very rarely in the courts, is dwelt on in grand language.

[The rest of Messala's speech is lost. Maternus is now again the speaker.]

CHAP. XXXVI.

Great eloquence, like fire, grows with its material; it becomes fiercer with movement, and brighter as it burns. On this same principle was developed in our state too the eloquence of antiquity. Although even the modern orator has attained all that the circumstances of a settled, quiet, and prosperous community allow, still in the disorder and licence of the past more seemed to be within the reach of the speaker, when, amid a universal confusion that needed one guiding hand, he exactly adapted his wisdom to the bewildered people's capacity of conviction. Hence, laws without end and consequent popularity; hence, speeches of magistrates who, I may say, passed nights on the Rostra; hence, prosecutions of influential citizens brought to trial, and feuds transmitted to whole families; hence, factions among the nobles, and incessant strife between the senate and the people. In each case the state was tôrn asunder, but the eloquence of the age was exercised and, as it seemed, was loaded with great rewards. For the more powerful a man was as a speaker, the more easily did he

CHAP. XXXVI. obtain office, the more decisively superior was he to his colleagues in office, the more influence did he acquire with the leaders of the state, the more weight in the senate, the more notoriety and fame with the people. Such men had a host of clients, even among foreign nations; the magistrates, when leaving Rome for the provinces, showed them respect, and courted their favour as soon as they returned. The prætorship and the consulship seemed to offer themselves to them, and even when they were out of office, they were not out of power, for they swayed both people and senate with their counsels and influence. Indeed, they had quite convinced themselves that without eloquence no one could win or retain a distinguished and eminent position in the state. And no wonder. Even against their own wish they had to show themselves before the people. It was little good for them to give a brief vote in the senate without supporting their opinion with ability and eloquence. If brought into popular odium, or under some charge, they had to reply in their own words. Again, they were under the necessity of giving evidence in the public courts, not in their absence by affidavit, but of being present and of speaking it openly. There was thus a strong stimulus to win the great prizes of eloquence, and as the reputation of a good speaker was considered an honour and a glory, so it was thought a disgrace to seem mute and speechless. Shame therefore quite as much as hope of reward prompted men not to take the place of a pitiful client rather than that of a patron, or to see hereditary connections transferred to others, or to seem spiritless and incapable of office from either failing to obtain it or from holding it weakly when obtained. CHAP XXXVI

CHAP XXXVII Perhaps you have had in your hands the old records, still to be found in the libraries of antiquaries, which Mucianus is just now collecting, and which have already been brought together and published in, I think, eleven books of Transactions, and three of Letters. From these we may gather that Cneius Pompeius and Marcus Crassus rose to power as much by force of intellect and by speaking as by their might in arms; that the Lentuli, Metelli, Luculli, and Curios, and the rest of our nobles, bestowed great labour and pains on these studies, and that, in fact, no one in those days acquired much influence without some eloquence. We must consider too the eminence of the men accused, and the vast issues involved. These of themselves do very much for eloquence. There is, indeed, a wide difference between having to speak on a theft, a technical point, a judicial decision, and on bribery at elections, the plundering of the allies, and the massacre of citizens. Though it is better that these evils should not befall us, and the best condition of the state is that in which we are spared such sufferings, still, when they did occur, they supplied a grand material for the orator. His mental powers rise with the dignity of his subject, and no one can produce a noble and brilliant speech unless he has got an adequate case. Demosthenes, I take it, does not owe his fame to his speeches against his guardians, and it is not his defence of Publius Quintius, or of Licinius Archias, which make Cicero a great orator; it is his Catiline, his Milo,

CHAP XXXVII his Verres, and Antonius, which have shed over him this lustre Not indeed that it was worth the state's while to endure bad citizens that orators might have plenty of matter for their speeches, but, as I now and then remind you, we must remember the point, and understand that we are speaking of an ait which arose more easily in stormy and unquiet times. Who knows not that it is better and more profitable to enjoy peace than to be harassed by war? Yet war produces more good soldiers than peace. Eloquence is on the same footing. The oftener she has stood, so to say, in the battle-field, the more wounds she has inflicted and received, the mightier her antagonist, the sharper the conflicts she has freely chosen, the higher and more splendid has been her rise, and ennobled by these contests she lives in the praises of mankind.

CHAP XXXVIII. I pass now to the forms and character of procedure in the old courts. As they exist now, they are indeed more favourable to truth, but the forum in those days was a better training for eloquence. There no speaker was under the necessity of concluding within a very few hours; there was freedom of adjournment, and every one fixed for himself the limits of his speech, and there was no prescribed number of days or of counsel. It was Cneius Pompeius who, in his third consulship, first restricted all this, and put a bridle, so to say, on eloquence, intending, however, that all business should be transacted in the forum according to law, and before the prætors. Here is a stronger proof of the greater importance of the cases tried before these judges than in the fact that causes in the Court of the Hundred, causes which now hold the first place, were then so eclipsed by the fame of other trials that not a speech of Cicero, or Cæsar, or Brutus, or Caelius, or Calvus, or, in short, any great orator is now read, that was delivered in that Court, except only the orations of Asinius Pollio for the heirs of Urbinia, as they are entitled, and even Pollio delivered these in the middle of the reign of Augustus, a period of long rest, of unbroken repose for the people and tranquillity for the senate, when the emperor's perfect discipline had put its restraints on eloquence as well as on all else. CHAP. XXXVIII.

Perhaps what I am going to say will be thought trifling and ridiculous; but I will say it even to be laughed at. What contempt (so I think at least) has been brought on eloquence by those little overcoats into which we squeeze, and, so to say, box ourselves up, when we chat with the judges! How much force may we suppose has been taken from our speeches by the little rooms and offices in which nearly all cases have to be set forth. Just as a spacious course tests a fine horse, so the orator has his field, and unless he can move in it freely and at ease, his eloquence grows feeble and breaks down. Nay more; we find the pains and labour of careful composition out of place, for the judge keeps asking when you are going to open the case, and you must begin from his question. Frequently he imposes silence on the advocate to hear proofs and witnesses. Meanwhile only one or two persons stand by you as you are CHAP XXXIX.

CHAP. XXXIX. speaking and the whole business is transacted almost in solitude. But the orator wants shouts and applause, and something like a theatre, all which and the like were the every day lot of the orators of antiquity, when both numbers and nobility pressed into the forum, when gatherings of clients and the people in their tribes and deputations from the towns and indeed a great part of Italy stood by the accused in his peril, and Rome's citizens felt in a multitude of trials that they themselves had an interest in the decision. We know that there was a universal rush of the people to hear the accusation and the defence of Cornelius, Scaurus, Milo, Bestia, and Vatinius, so that even the coldest speaker might have been stirred and kindled by the mere enthusiasm of the citizens in their strife. And therefore indeed such pleadings are still extant, and thus the men too who pleaded, owe their fame to no other speeches more than these.

CHAP. XL. Again, what stimulus to genius and what fire to the orator was furnished by incessant popular assemblies, by the privilege of attacking the most influential men, and by the very glory of such feuds when most of the good speakers did not spare even a Publius Scipio, or a Sulla, or a Cneius Pompeius, and following the common impulse of envy availed themselves of the popular ear for invective against eminent citizens. I am not speaking of a quiet and peaceful accomplishment, which delights in what is virtuous and well regulated. No; the great and famous eloquence of old is the nursling of the licence which fools called freedom; it is the companion of sedition, the stimulant of an unruly people, a stranger to obedience and subjection, a defiant, reckless, presumptuous thing which does not show itself in a well-governed state. What orator have we ever heard of at Sparta or at Crete? A very strict discipline and very strict laws prevailed, tradition says, in both those states. Nor do we know of the existence of eloquence among the Macedonians or Persians, or in any people content with a settled government. There were some orators at Rhodes and a host of them at Athens, but there the people, there any ignorant follow, anybody, in short, could do anything. So too our own state, while it went astray and wore out its strength in factious strife and discord, with neither peace in the forum, unity in the senate, order in the courts, respect for merit, or seemly behaviour in the magistrates, produced beyond all question a more vigorous eloquence, just as an untilled field yields certain herbage in special plenty. Still the eloquence of the Gracchi was not an equivalent to Rome for having to endure their legislation, and Cicero's fame as an orator was a poor compensation for the death he died. CHAP XL.

And so now the forum, which is all that our speakers have left them of antiquity, is an evidence of a state not thoroughly reformed or as orderly as we could wish. Who but the guilty or unfortunate apply to us? What town puts itself under our protection but one harassed by its neighbours or by strife at home? When we plead for a province, is it not one that has been plundered and ill-treated? Surely it would be better not to complain than to have to seek CHAP. XLI.

CHAP XLI

redress. Could a community be found in which no one did wrong, an orator would be as superfluous among its innocent people as a physician among the healthy. As the healing art is of very little use and makes very little progress in nations which enjoy particularly robust constitutions and vigorous frames, so the orator gets an inferior and less splendid renown where a sound morality and willing obedience to authority prevail. What need there of long speeches in the senate, when the best men are soon of one mind, or of endless harangues to the people, when political questions are decided not by an ignorant multitude, but by one man of pre-eminent wisdom? What need of voluntary prosecutions, when crimes are so rare and slight, or of defences full of spiteful insinuation and exceeding proper bounds, when the clemency of the judge offers itself to the accused in his peril?

Be assured, my most excellent, and, as far as the age requires, most eloquent friends, that had you been born in the past, and the men we admire in our own day, had some god in fact suddenly changed your lives and your age, the highest fame and glory of eloquence would have been yours, and they too would not have lacked moderation and self-control. As it is, seeing that no one can at the same time enjoy great renown and great tranquillity, let everybody make the best of the blessings of his own age without disparaging other periods.

Maternus had now finished. There were, replied Messala, some points I should controvert, some on which I should like to hear more, if the day were not almost spent. It shall be, said Maternus, as you wish, on a future occasion, and anything you have thought obscure in my argument, we will again discuss. Then he rose and embraced Aper. I mean, he said, to accuse you before the poets, and so will Messala before the antiquarians. And I, rejoined Aper, will accuse you before the rhetoricians and professors. CHAP. XLI.

They laughed good-humouredly, and we parted.

NOTES TO THE

DIALOGUE ON ORATORY.

CHAP. V. *Saleius Bassus.*—Mentioned again in 9 and 10. He was a poet of the Flavian age, of whom Quintilian (x. 1. 90) speaks favourably, as possessed of a *vehemens et poeticum ingenium.* Juvenal (vii. 80) gives him the epithet *tenuis*, in allusion, it would seem, to his poverty. There is extant a panegyrical poem of 261 lines on a Calpurnius Piso, and this has been attributed to Bassus, it being also supposed that this Piso was one of the chief authors of the famous conspiracy against Nero, described in the Annals xv. 48 to end. The conjecture is a plausible one, but that is all that can be said of it. There were many other poets who may have written it, as, for example Statius or Lucan.

CHAP. VII. *Ministers of the crown* (*procuratores principum*). —The *procurator Cæsaris*, as he was styled was commonly the emperor's confidential adviser as well as his steward. He could have a province if he wished it, as a matter of course. When impeached, it would usually be for extortion or maladministration. He was often a freedman, and his class with its peculiar influence was one of the most marked features of the imperial age. CHAP. VII.

Mandate (*codicillis*).—Compare Agricola 40, where the same word *codicilli* is used of a dispatch or missive from the emperor to Agricola. This indeed seems to have become one of the *special* meanings of the word, which properly, of course, is simply a diminutive form of *codex*.

Men with the tunic (*tunicatus populus*)—Compare Horace Epist. i. 7, 65, *tunicato popello*. A respectable Roman citizen always wore the *toga* in public; to be without this and have only the *tunica* implied that a man belonged to the poorest and lowest class. The *tunica* was worn under the *toga*.

CHAP. VIII.

Eprius Marcellus.—First mentioned in Annals xii. 4. He rose from obscurity by the abuse of considerable natural eloquence to be one of the foremost *delatores* of Nero's time, during which he was particularly formidable. He lost influence after Nero's death, but reappears in Hist. ii 53; iv. 6. and was an important personage under Vitellius and Vespasian.

Vibius Crispus.—He is again mentioned in 13. He had successfully defended his brother in Nero's reign on a charge of provincial maladministration. See Annals xiv. 28. Quintilian (x. 1, 119) speaks of him as *jucundus et delectationi natus*. See also Hist. ii. 10; iv. 41, 43.

CHAP. IX

Programmes (*libellos*).—Perhaps, cards of invitation with a programme. Juvenal (vii. 35—97), describes at length the process of getting up a reading and drawing an audience.

Vatinius.—See Annals xv. 34, from which it

CHAP IX. appears that from having been a shoemaker's apprentice he had pushed himself into Nero's favour by vulgar wit and buffoonery. How Maternus "broke his power" and drove him from the court we cannot say, as Tacitus tells us nothing about it. It hardly seems likely that he won a victory over him in a tragedy contest, as Gronovius conjectured. Such solemn contests would not have been very congenial to Nero's taste or to that of the people, nor was Vatinius the sort of man to write a tragedy. Ritter discusses this passage in a long excursus, in which he throws out the conjecture that Maternus's tragedy of Domitius, mentioned in 3, was identical with that referred to in the present passage. It was, he thinks, a tragedy based on an incident said to have occurred to Nero in his infancy, which Tacitus glances at in Annals xi 11. ("It was commonly reported that snakes had been seen by his cradle which they seemed to guard.") Nero's name indeed was Domitius, but it is not easy to see why Maternus should have so called him, as after his adoption in early years by the Emperor Claudius he was known as Claudius Nero. He would too have been much too young to have been the leading character of a tragedy. There remains something in this passage which cannot be cleared up. We know nothing of the circumstances under which Vatinius lost the Emperor's favour; we may infer perhaps from Hist. i 37 that in Otho's time he was dead.

CHAP XIII *The pallors of fame* (*famam pallentem*).—A pale face goes with fame, as it does with study. The man who has it, fears for himself as much as he is feared by others.

CHAP. XIV.

Julius Asiaticus.—Probably the same man as the Asiaticus mentioned Hist. ii. 94; if so, he had taken a leading part in the insurrection of Vindex. He was a Gaul, or born in Gaul, and this explains the fact that Julius Secundus, himself of Gallic origin, had written his life.

CHAP. XV

Nicetes.—A rhetoric-professor in the time of Claudius and Nero. He taught both at Rome and at Smyrna, his native city. The younger Pliny (vi. 6) had attended his lectures, and speaks of him as a particularly earnest student (*studiorum amantissimus*).

Africanus.—A son probably of the Julius Africanus mentioned in the Annals vi. 7. He lived in Nero's time. Quintilian couples him with Afer as a distinguished orator.

CHAP. XVII.

Menenius Agrippa.—He led the famous secession of the *plebs* to *Mons Sacer* in 492 B.C. See Livy ii 32.

Caelius.—Marcus Caelius Rufus, a friend of Cicero and defended him in the famous speech *Pro Caelio.*

Calvus.—Caius Licinius Calvus, also a contemporary of Cicero, both a poet and orator. As the first he ranked with Catullus; as the latter with Cicero. He had also the name of Macer, and it is not unlikely that he was the Licinius Macer so often referred to by Livy. Of his works only the merest scraps remain.

Hirtius and Pansa.—They were consuls in 43 B.C., and both fell in that year, which came to be henceforth regarded as marking the end of the commonwealth.

CHAP XVIII *Appius Caecus.*—His speech on the subject of a treaty with Pyrrhus in 280 B.C. was, it appears, extant in Cicero's time (see the Brutus, 16), and may have been known to Tacitus.

CHAP XIX. *Cassius Severus.*—His career is briefly sketched in Annals iv. 21.

CHAP XX *Roscius or Ambivius.*—The first was a highly accomplished tragic actor, and was a particular favourite with Sulla and with Cicero. One of Cicero's speeches is in his defence. Ambivius was a comic actor in the time of Terence, and had a great reputation.

CHAP. XXI. *Canutius.*—Mentioned by Cicero in his speech for Cluentius (10) and in the Brutus (56) as a very good speaker.

Vatinius.—One of Cæsar's most active adherents and, as such, a conspicuous figure in the strife between Cæsar and Pompeius.

CHAP XXIII. *Aufidius Bassus*—A writer in the time of Augustus and Tiberius. He wrote a history of the German war.

Servilius Nonianus.—See Annals xiv. 19, from which it appears that he was eminent as a counsel and as a historian.

Sisenna.—Mentioned by Cicero (Brutus 64), as a clever but not sufficiently careful writer. He wrote a history of Sulla's times.

Varro.—The learned writer and student of antiquity whose great work was known as *De vita populi Romani et de antiquitatibus rerum humanarum et divinarum*

Maecenas.—Horace and Virgil's patron. Tacitus here describes his style of eloquence by a phrase borrowed from Cicero's Brutus (75), *calamistri* (curling-irons). CHAP. XXVI.

Gallio.—Lucius Junius Gallio, Seneca's adopted father, who lived in the time of Augustus.

Quintus Mucius.—Surnamed Scaevola *pontifex maximus*, and a famous jurist, a man whom Cicero greatly and deservedly admired. His merit was that he first treated Roman law scientifically. He was murdered B.C. 82, by the order of the younger Marius. CHAP. XXX.

Philo.—He was at the head of the academy in Cicero's time. Cicero says (Tusc. ii. 3) that he had often heard him.

Diodotus.—He was a personal friend of Cicero, by whom he was very much esteemed. In fact, he had taught Cicero as a boy. See Tusc. v. 39; Epist ad Fam. xiii. 16.

Asia.—We must understand Asia Minor, not merely the Roman province so called.

Good and evil, &c. (*bonis ac malis, honesto et turpi*). —These are here *philosophical* terms, as in Cicero's *De Finibus Bonorum et Malorum.* The same applies to several expressions in this chapter. CHAP. XXXI

Human nature.—This has quite a modern tone, which deserves to be noted. It would be difficult to find a passage in which *humana natura* answered so closely to its English equivalent.

The biassed (*cupidos*).—This is probably the meaning, *cupidus* being specially used to denote undue favour or partiality in a hearer or a judge.

CHAP XXXIV *Success or failure.*—There is probably something wrong here in the text, which is simply *ut nec bene dicta dissimularentur.* Orelli thinks that the words *nec male* must have dropped out, and we have so translated. Ritter is satisfied with the text as it stands, and takes the meaning to be "that good speaking is not denied to be such even by unfriendly critics," because, as has been above explained, the speaker is notoriously subjected to very hard conditions. He wants to make *nec bene* equivalent to *ne bene quidem* but this seems questionable, and if admitted, the sense remains obscure.

In his nineteenth year.—This is an error; Lucius Crassus was in his twenty-first year when he impeached Carbo for having undertaken to defend Opimius, the murderer of Caius Gracchus.

In his twenty-first year.—Another error; Cæsar was in his twenty-third year at the time. The Dolabella whom Cæsar prosecuted was the father of Publius Dolabella, Cicero's son-in-law. The charge against him was for extortion (*repetundae*) in his province of Macedonia. He was defended by Hortensius and acquitted.

CHAP XXXV *School of Impudence.*—The expression occurs in Cicero, de Oratore iii. 24.

CHAP XXXVII. *Hereditary connexions* (*traditae a majoribus necessitudines*).—A lawyer's business, as we know, is frequently hereditary, and we gather from this passage that it was so at Rome.

Mucianus.—The Licinius Crassus Mucianus, who materially helped Vespasian to empire. We may conjecture that the literary collection which he is here said to have made under the title of *Actorum libri* comprised selections from the speeches of eminent men with summaries of the cases in which they were engaged.

Urbinia.—In this case one Clusinius Figulus after Urbinia's decease represented himself to be her son, and claimed her property. He had long been in foreign parts, and at last returned to make his claim, which, however, he was unable to make good. Asinius Pollio was counsel for the heirs, and he proved to the satisfaction of the judges that the claimant was really a slave, by name Sosipater. CHAP XXXVIII

Cornelius.—Defended by Cicero B C. 65 on a charge of *majestas.* CHAP. XXXIX

Scaurus, Milo, Bestia, Vatinius.—All these too were defended by Cicero in the years B.C. 54, 52, 56 and 54. The speech for Milo is still extant; the other speeches are lost, with the exception of some fragments of the speech for Scaurus.

Rhodes.—Apollonius Molo was the most famous of the orators of Rhodes. Cicero studied under him, and highly valued his teaching. See his Brutus (91). CHAP. XL.

LONDON
R. CLAY, SONS AND TAYLOR,
BREAD STREET HILL, E.C.

MESSRS. MACMILLAN AND CO.'S

CLASSICAL PUBLICATIONS.

TRANSLATIONS.

ARISTOTLE.—THE POLITICS. Translated by Rev. J. E. C. WELLDON, M.A. Crown 8vo. 10*s* 6*d*.

THE RHETORIC. By the same Translator. [*In preparation.*

CICERO.—THE ACADEMICS. Translated by J. S. REID, M.L. 8vo 5*s* 6*d*

SELECT LETTERS. After the Edition of ALBERT WATSON, M.A. Translated by G. E. JEANS, M.A. 8vo 10*s* 6*d*.

HOMER.—THE ILIAD. Translated into English Prose. By ANDREW LANG, M.A., WALTER LEAF, M.A., and ERNEST MYERS, M.A. Crown 8vo. 12*s* 6*d*.

THE ODYSSEY. Done into English by Professor S. H. BUTCHER, M.A., and ANDREW LANG, M.A. Fourth Edition, revised and corrected. Crown 8vo. 10*s* 6*d*.

HORACE.—THE WORKS OF HORACE RENDERED INTO ENGLISH PROSE With Introductions, Running Analysis, Notes, &c. By J. LONSDALE, M.A., and S. LEE, M.A. (*Globe Edition*) 3*s* 6*d*

THIRTEEN SATIRES. Translated into English after the Text of J. E. B. MAYOR by Professor HERBERT STRONG, M.A., and ALEXANDER LEEPER, M.A. Crown 8vo 3*s* 6*d*

LIVY. BOOKS XXI.—XXV. Translated by ALFRED JOHN CHURCH, M.A., and WILLIAM JACKSON BRODRIBB, M.A. Crown 8vo 7*s* 6*d*.

PINDAR.—THE EXTANT ODES OF PINDAR. Translated into English, with an Introduction and short Notes, by ERNEST MYERS, M.A. Second Edition Crown 8vo. 5*s*.

PLATO.—THE REPUBLIC OF PLATO. Translated into English, with an Analysis and Notes, by J. LL. DAVIES, M.A., and D. J. VAUGHAN, M.A. 18mo 4*s*. 6*d*

EUTHYPHRO, APOLOGY, CRITO, AND PHÆDO. Translated by F. J. CHURCH Crown 8vo 4*s* 6*d*.

SALLUST.—CATILINE AND JUGURTHA. Translated, with Introductory Essays, by A. W. POLLARD, B.A. Crown 8vo. 6*s*.

MACMILLAN AND CO., LONDON.

Lightning Source UK Ltd.
Milton Keynes UK
UKHW022114300522
403744UK00003B/291

9 781360 148168